PENGUIN BOOKS

Don't You Love Your Daddy?

PENGUIN BOOKS

Published by the Penguin Group
Penguin Books Ltd, 80 Strand, London WC2R ORL, England
Penguin Group (USA) Inc., 375 Hudson Street, New York, New York 10014, USA
Penguin Group (Canada), 90 Eglinton Avenue East, Suite 700, Toronto, Ontario, Canada M4P 2Y3
(a division of Pearson Penguin Canada Inc.)
Penguin Ireland, 25 St Stephen's Green, Dublin 2, Ireland (a division of Penguin Books Ltd)
Penguin Group (Australia), 250 Camberwell Road, Camberwell, Victoria 3124, Australia
(a division of Pearson Australia Group Pty Ltd)
Penguin Books India Pvt Ltd, 11 Community Centre, Panchsheel Park, New Delhi – 110 017, India
Penguin Group (NZ), 67 Apollo Drive, Rosedale, North Shore 0632, New Zealand
(a division of Pearson New Zealand Ltd)
Penguin Books (South Africa) (Pty) Ltd, 24 Sturdee Avenue, Rosebank, Johannesburg 2196, South Africa

Penguin Books Ltd, Registered Offices: 80 Strand, London WC2R ORL, England

www.penguin.com

First published 2010

2

Set in 12.5/14.75 Garamond MT Std
Typeset by TexTech International
Printed in England by Clays Ltd, St Ives plc

ISBN: 978-0-718-19228-0

www.greenpenguin.co.uk

Mixed Sources
Product group from well-managed
forests and other controlled sources
www.fsc.org Cert no. SA-COC-1592
© 1996 Forest Stewardship Council

Penguin Books is committed to a sustainable future
for our business, our readers and our planet.
The book in your hands is made from paper
certified by the Forest Stewardship Council.

I have never visited my father's grave. I know where it is, of course, for when he died I had received a phone call inviting me to his funeral. An invitation I chose to ignore – I had no need to say my final goodbyes: they had been said a long time before.

Over the years since I learnt of his death I have tried to erase all memories of him from my thoughts, but still they slither unwanted into my mind – as does the image of the small blonde-haired, green-eyed child who once was me.

I see her when, scarcely older than a toddler, she loved her tall, handsome, dark-haired father. When, returning from his work as a carpenter, he bounced into the house with a wide smile that she thought was just for her, she would stretch her arms towards him, her face alight with joy at his return. Even before her chubby little hands received the sweets or bars of chocolate that she knew he would have hidden in his jacket pocket especially for her, she would demand his immediate attention. 'Up, Daddy, uppy!' she would urge him.

And, laughing at her determination, he would sweep her up from the floor and swing her into the air. I can still hear his voice murmuring, 'You're my own special little girl, aren't you, Sally?' Her arms would wind around his neck – she liked the feel of him holding her. She enjoyed inhaling his particular aroma, one of newly sawed timber, wood varnish, cigarettes and aftershave that clung to his skin, hair and clothes. With his rough cheek pressed to hers, she snuggled against his chest.

'Don't you love your daddy?' he would ask, and always received a fast succession of nods in reply. 'Well, say it, then!' he would demand, and obediently she would utter the words he wanted to hear.

'I love you, Daddy.'

That was before she began to fear him.

Chapter One

The first seven years of my life were spent in a northern English village where, from spring to late autumn, children played in the streets and women stood outside shops or leant over garden fences chatting. When October, with its thin drizzling rain, gave way to November, iron-grey clouds released sheets of rain, hail and sleet. Then we hurried back to our houses and scuttled inside for warmth. During the months before spring arrived, the dark streets were almost deserted as people huddled inside their homes. The flickering lights of televisions shone out of dim rooms and fell on the bare branches of trees, while soggy clumps of fallen leaves drifted in the gutters. Early evening brought the sound of slamming doors, which announced the men returning from work. Their battered old cars lined the streets, for in the country, apart from a daily bus, they were the only means of transport other than bicycles.

The house I was born into was a three-bedroom terrace in the middle of a council estate that lay on the edge of our village. My mother told me that when, ten years before I was born, my parents had moved in, the houses smelt of new paint and recently dried plaster. The small gardens, bisected by a short concrete path, were freshly dug farm soil: no grass had been laid, no shrubs or flowers planted.

For many of the young couples who had been handed a front-door key, it was their first home; they had lived with parents or in-laws while they waited for a council house to become available. But the one thing that every family moving on to the new estate shared was optimism.

By the time I was old enough to notice the difference between our house and the others on the estate, the years of neglect had taken their toll. Paint had peeled off the window and door frames, and while our neighbours' gardens had been lovingly nurtured, ours was overgrown with coarse grass and dead bushes. The wind brought seeds that took root sometimes, but finally withered and died.

Apart from the times when my mother seemed to have unlimited energy, our curtains hung drably from the windows, while in the backyard damp washing, which often she left out for days, flapped on a sagging rope clothes-line.

My elder brother, Pete, was a baby of only a few months when they moved in, but by the time I was old enough to know him, he was an angry teenager who avoided his home and, it appeared, me too.

My father's family, which consisted of three brothers, their wives and children, his unmarried sister and my grand-parents, all lived in the village, and as a small child I always had my cousins of various ages to play with. My mother had only one sister, Janet, who lived nearly a hundred miles away. I don't remember my maternal grandparents, who were already middle-aged when their two daughters were born, as they had died when I was just a baby.

Every Sunday our whole family would meet at the

church, the men in dark suits and the women wearing matching Crimplene dresses and jackets, with an assortment of hats, while the children had on their Sunday best. Young boys wore short trousers, crisp white shirts, their school ties and blazers, and their hair was combed neatly into place. The girls were smart in skirts, blouses and jumpers. I can remember that I wore, depending on the season, either a plaid dress or a pink cotton one, with short white lacy socks and black patent shoes; Pete wore long grey flannel trousers and a dark blue blazer.

When my mother came to church dressed in something long and floaty made of brightly coloured Indian cotton, she looked different from the other women. With her shiny shoulder-length blonde hair uncovered, her porcelain skin and slender figure, I thought she was the prettiest mother there. I liked it when she was beside me in church, her hand wrapped around my smaller one, and I felt something akin to shame for her when she failed to make an appearance. 'Too tired,' was one of her excuses or 'Not feeling well,' and before we left the house without her I would see my father's face tighten with barely concealed rage.

'What do you think it looks like you not being there?' he would ask, but she only shrugged and muttered that she didn't really care.

'Your mother will give you all your Sunday lunch,' she said, in a faraway voice. 'She likes to do that.' My father would stomp out of the house, with me and Pete following anxiously behind him.

When the assembled family saw that, once again, my mother had not come with us, there was an exasperated sigh from my stern grandfather and tutting from my grandmother who, with my aunts, uncles and cousins, were impatiently waiting on the church steps for us to arrive.

My grandmother's hand would rest briefly on my shoulder to show it was not me she was angry with, before we all trooped inside to take our places.

Too young to read the hymns I had managed to learn the words of the most popular ones and sang along enthusiastically. I loved the beauty of the church, with its high arches and stained-glass windows, the pure sounds of the organ and the choir, but I was always bored by the sermon. It made little sense to me and just seemed to go on and on. I tried not to fidget but it was hard to sit still, and Pete also appeared bored and tried to make me giggle by pulling funny faces. If my father saw him and glared, he would cast his eyes down and slouch on the pew.

'You'd better come to my house for your Sunday roast,' my grandmother would say, each time my mother failed to put in an appearance. Her mouth, devoid of lipstick, pursed in disapproval at what she saw as her daughter-in-law's neglect of her wifely duties. She sniffed loudly and added, 'I doubt Laura's prepared anything.' Which, of course, my mother hadn't, and as the men in our village thought it was something special if they made a cup of tea, it was unlikely that my father would cook our lunch.

My grandmother's Sunday lunches seldom varied – 'Men expect to eat a roast whatever the weather does,' she always said. So, regardless of the season, a large joint of roast beef would be placed before my grandfather for him to carve, and the table was covered with jugs of onion gravy, dishes of crisp roast potatoes, a selection of vegetables and a platter of golden Yorkshire puddings. Plates were piled high, second helpings were offered, and thick slices of apple tart or spoonfuls of fruit crumble covered with custard were passed round.

I liked going to my grandmother's house, where mouth-watering smells drifted from her sparkling kitchen. In her home I was always made a fuss of, but I didn't like hearing disparaging remarks about my mother.

'So she's not well again?' I would hear my aunt say to my father, before my grandmother could tell her not to talk about it in front of me. Several censorious sniffs would follow until she was unable to keep her thoughts to herself. 'I'd like to know what Laura's got wrong in her life to make her feel so sorry for herself. There's you in a good job – with all this building of new estates round here, a carpenter will always be in work. You live in a nice house and have two lovely children. She never wants for anything, does she? She needs a bit of firmness, that one does. You're just too soft for your own good, David, and it's a bad example for young Sally and Pete as well.'

The deep depressions that dogged my mother were viewed with little tolerance – 'bipolar', or 'manic depression', as it was more often called then, was not an illness that was widely recognized and my mother's 'bad days' received scant sympathy from my father's female relatives. Women's Liberation and, with it, the knowledge of the various physical and mental problems that beset women might have started in the sixties, but during my childhood, it still hadn't knocked on any doors in our working-class northern village. Like their mothers before them, these married women seldom went out to work: instead they believed that their role in life was to keep a clean house, cook tasty meals, and bring up their children in the manner that they had been raised. My mother's inability to do those tasks consistently was frowned upon, and her mood swings were put down to laziness and ingratitude.

On Sundays, which my father referred to as 'our Lord's day', we were not allowed to play in the street or the play areas on our estate. 'It's disrespectful to the Lord,' my father would state firmly. So, once lunch was finished, I sat on the sitting-room floor and coloured in picture books or watched television if there was an old black and white film on. From time to time my eyes would drift longingly to the street outside: I could hear children playing and I'd wish I could join them. But I knew I would be refused permission should I ask.

When we returned to our house, often it was to find it in darkness with my mother asleep on the settee and the fire my father had lit that morning gone out.

Chapter Two

Our home was a place where shouts followed by shrieks and muffled sobs were heard constantly. Their consistency gave them a veneer of normality, and over the years, as I grew from toddler to small child, they became woven into the fabric of my life. My father seldom tried to hide his impatience or lower his voice when he was confronted with what he thought were his wife's imaginary illnesses. Too often I overheard him shout, 'Pull yourself together, Laura.' For days at a time she seemed incapable of doing that.

I learnt when I was about three that what my mother called her 'black days' made her cry, but I seldom questioned why. I only knew that the noises of her unhappiness and my father's frustration frightened me. At night when the sounds of their anger and despair carried up the stairs and into my room, I would lie in bed with my fingers stuffed into my ears, praying for them to stop.

At fourteen Pete was at the gangly, sulky stage, with a voice that squeaked one moment and was a deep bass the next. When he heard my father erupting into red-faced, fist-waving fury, he would glare at him and storm out of the house. The sound of the back door banging was his only way of showing how upset he was. I wished I could have followed him but I was too young. Instead I just curled up tighter. With my stomach churning, I waited for the shouting to cease.

Over the years, my memories of my mother have merged into one large photographic collage that I have hung in my mind to look at when I think back to how it was then. Some are blurred, as if faded with age, but others are still sharp and clear. I cannot put in order all my memories, but I do know that every one of my mother and the time I spent with her occurred before I was six and a half.

I know, because that was when everything changed.

As a small child I learnt to recognize my mother's extreme mood swings: warm smiles when I awoke heralded a good day. 'Come on, up you get, lazybones,' she would say, as she tickled my stomach, then pulled me out of bed. On good days she would brush my pale blonde hair. 'Such beautiful hair – you must never cut it short,' she would say, as she tied it into bunches or drew it back from my face with a black velvet hairband.

'It's like yours, Mummy,' I replied, for my mother's hair was the colour of the corn that was harvested in the autumn.

'Mine's not as pretty,' she would say, then dress me and take me downstairs for breakfast.

I can still see her on warm sunny days, in a long denim skirt and a red and black crocheted waistcoat she had made for herself. She always tucked her shoulder-length hair behind her ears when, in a whirl of frantic activity, she cleaned the house from top to bottom. Her green eyes sparkled mischievously as she changed bedding, vacuumed the carpets, cleaned windows and washed the net curtains, stained yellow by the cigarettes she had smoked. Everything smelt of bleach and polish. Scatter cushions were plumped on the Dralon lounge suite, old magazines and newspapers were thrown out and everything was put away until nothing was out of place.

On those days it was just the two of us alone until my brother returned from school and my father from work. Once the housework was done we would spend our time playing games or my mother would sit me next to her on the settee, her arm around my shoulders as she read me stories. Noddy and his friend Big Ears came to life for me as did Snow White and her Seven Dwarfs. Sometimes my mother would make up her own stories where I was the central character and heroine. They were always about meeting fairies, friendly dragons and laughing giants – and it was those tales that I loved most.

On other good days we would spend the whole afternoon painting and drawing. My mother would put big colouring books on the table and drape a protective cloth over my dress. While I was absorbed in splashing bright colours on to the paper she baked cakes and biscuits, giving me the mixing bowl to scrape out. I would watch the oven out of the corner of my eye: she would give me a biscuit the moment it was cool enough to hold.

There were times when my mother, having spotted a new recipe in a magazine and eager to try it out, would dash to the shops for the ingredients. When she got home the table was soon covered with bowls, as vegetables were expertly diced, meat chopped and cream whisked. 'Sally, we must lay the table properly,' she would say, after one of those rare frenetic cooking bouts. The dinner service, which had been a wedding present, would be unearthed from the sideboard and washed. Small pieces of silver – a jug, some spoons, a salt cellar – also came out. I was given the task of dipping a cloth in the silver polish and rubbing away the tarnish that had stained them since the last time they had been used. I liked the rough gritty feel of the pink paste on my fingers when I helped her remove the dark stains and admired the gleam of each piece when we had polished it.

On those evenings my father would smile as he walked through the door and remark on the clean house and the cooking smells. Even Pete would sit down and eat with us instead of grabbing a snack and disappearing to his room under the pretext of having homework to finish. With my parents seemingly relaxed in each other's company, we appeared to have become a normal family. On my mother's good days I was content: she was the mother I loved and, for a short time, I could believe that the interlude would last – but it never did.

Chapter Three

Near our house there was a play area for the children, and during the summer my mother and I would often spend mornings there. The swings were the first thing I headed for and I would beg my mother to push harder to make me go higher. With my legs stretched out and my head tipped back, I shrieked with delight when the swing rose higher and higher. Up there, I could see neighbours hanging out washing, children playing and teenagers sunbathing. When my mother had had enough of pushing me, we would go to the seesaw where she bounced me up and down.

On the down days, when my mother ignored my pleas to go to the play area because she was too tired to take me, I was confined to our small garden and left there to amuse myself. My bright red Space Hopper was brought out and I would bounce up and down on the broken concrete path for hours.

I thought that I must have caused my mother's unhappiness – I couldn't understand why she was so unhappy on some days and so happy on others. Maybe, I thought, it was the unsightly red spots of my eczema, which had appeared soon after I was born, but I never found the courage to ask her.

'You're a beautiful little girl,' she told me on her good days, but by the time I started school I had ceased to believe her.

I can only imagine how my mother felt when the midwife placed me in her arms for the first time – after all, that is her memory, not mine, one that she polished with love, for that is what mothers do, before sharing it with me. 'I loved you the moment I saw you,' she told me. 'With your fuzz of blonde hair and those big eyes of yours, you were a gorgeous baby.'

Well, maybe I was to her, but each time she tried to re-assure me I thought about my eczema. It covered my arms, crept up my neck and speckled my chest, and I thought of how I must have looked, with my baby face scrunched up and my skin marred by those angry red spots. Ever since I was a tiny tot I had heard the comments of well-intentioned people. Walking by my mother's side, her hand wrapped firmly round my tiny one lest I stumbled or fell, I heard neighbours and friends ask about my health and how my eczema was. Gazing up at them, I asked them silently to bend down to my height and ask me, but they never did. It was as though those ugly red spots rendered me both invisible and deaf.

'Will that rash get better?' they would ask. 'Does it hurt her?' And: 'Will it clear up when she's older?'

Each time they stopped my mother and put their questions to her, I felt her fingers grip my hand a little tighter. 'Of course it'll clear up,' she always said. 'It's just a children's thing.'

As I grew, the questions continued, but still they never asked me. If they had I could have told them that, yes, it hurt, that I hated those red spots and the itching, but they never did, so I never told them.

Every day my mother had to smooth cream, which

helped soothe my skin, over my body – 'Even when you were just a tiny baby and I had to rub it in, you were so good,' my mother told me. 'You never cried.' But I thought I must have.

At night my nails were trimmed, and when the rash spread and nearly my whole body was raw, she tied little white mittens over my hands to stop me scratching. My grandmother invented another way to stop me rubbing my rash when it spread over my arms: she cut open Fairy Liquid containers, removed their tops and bottoms, put my arms into them and taped them on.

'It won't get better if you scratch it, so this is to help you,' she told me, when tears of pain and self-pity ran down my face. She took a boiled sweet out of her handbag, unwrapped it and popped it into my mouth.

'Come, Sally, give your nana a kiss,' she would demand and I, standing on tiptoe, would raise matchstick arms, encased in their ugly covering, place them round her neck and reluctantly press my lips to her dry, papery skin.

I hated how I looked even more than the feeling of my arms being stiff and unwieldy. On warm days, when I wore a short-sleeved dress, I didn't want to leave the house and walk to the shops or the park with my mother. I was aware of the pity on her friends' faces and the curious stares from other children, and nothing she said reassured me, although she told me she loved me and that my rash didn't matter.

Chapter Four

On my mother's black days she didn't seem to notice me or even acknowledge my existence. There was no smiling face looking down at me when I awoke so I would climb out of bed and, still in my nightdress, go in search of her. Sometimes she was still in bed, a huddled shape hidden under the blankets; at others she was in the sitting room lying on the settee, her face turned to the wall. Frightened by her remoteness, I would sit silently, watching her, wishing she would wake up.

Those days seemed to accelerate the spread of my eczema, and as the dreaded itching began, my body twitched and I was unable to control my fingers. They would scratch until the skin on the back of my knees started to crack, weep and bleed, while my hands broke out in a mass of runny sores. It was not until I cried with pain that my mother's eyes would open. When she saw what her neglect had done, guilt would penetrate the dark fog of her depression. Raising herself up, she would wrap her arms around me, croon comforting words into my ears, and my face would be damp with her tears.

On those terrible days her hair hung limply around a pale, puffy face streaked with the constant tears that trickled down it. When she held me I would smell the sweet, cloying odour of stale apples that clung to her breath. It was a smell I learnt to recognize, and I knew it came from the pale frothy liquid she drank from the large brown bottles I watched her trying to hide from my father and Pete.

I was too young to understand the feelings that engulfed her on those days, the utter hopelessness that turned her from a pretty, vivacious woman into one I hardly knew.

It was not until I grew up and entered a place where I too sat staring into space, with tears running down my face as unwanted memories filled my mind, that I began to understand how my mother must have felt. Then, as I remembered her sitting on the settee with her head in her stiff fingers, I could identify with the despair that had flooded her and robbed her of all rational thought. I would watch her grasping and twisting her skirt, while her eyes stared at something only she could see. And when those memories came back and I looked down, my own hands were mimicking hers.

Then I would think of the little girl I had been, watching my mother gaze out at the darkness beyond the window until all I could see was the back of a head and the reflection of my mother's white face in the glass. My five-year-old self had thought it was as though a wicked witch had jumped out of a fairytale and cast a dark spell over her, and I wished that a good fairy would come and break it. Fear gnawed at me constantly then; fear that the mother I loved was lost to me for ever.

It was on those days that washing-up piled up in the sink, meals were missed or food was hastily prepared out of tins and packets, and my daily bath, followed by the cream, was forgotten.

Then there were no sounds of laughter in the house.

Instead it was filled with angry shouts when my father returned home from work. 'Oh, for God's sake! Not again! Pull yourself together, Laura,' he would yell, when he saw her sitting morosely on a chair or lying on the settee. Frightened, I would keep as quiet as I could.

It was during my mother's black days that my fear of my father started. When I was very small, maybe only three or four, it was just a bubble of unease that, over the months and years, grew little by little, but it wasn't until I was a teenager that my love for him was completely destroyed.

'Come, Sally,' my father would say, once I had eaten the supper he had cooked for me. 'I'll put you to bed. Your mother's in no fit state to do it.'

I was lifted up and placed in a tepid bath. I liked the feel of the water on my inflamed skin and the soapy flannel being wiped gently over me. But I didn't like it when it was moved to between my legs and I felt his fingers touching me there. Nor did I like what happened next. I would be picked up and, with a soft towel wrapped around my shoulders, sat on his knee, pulled close to his chest.

When I felt something hard pressing into my bottom I would try to wriggle away from him, only to feel his arms tighten and hear 'No,' whispered urgently into my ear. 'Stay still and let me rub your cream in, Sally,' he would say, when I squirmed in protest as his hands applied cream to parts that my eczema did not reach.

When tears spilled over and ran down my cheeks, they were wiped tenderly away. 'Whatever's wrong, Sally? You're getting as bad as your mother. Don't you love your daddy?' and, of course, I did – then. A kiss would be pressed to my cheek, a sweet popped into my mouth and he was back to being the father I loved.

As I grew a little older, my father began to exercise more and more control over me. In front of my grandparents and my mother, he would sit me on his knee, his hand stroking my legs. 'She's a daddy's girl, all right. Aren't you, Sally?' he would say. I wanted to twist myself out of his grasp and get down on the floor but, fearing his displeasure, I remained where I was.

His embraces when he returned home from work became tighter and more frequent, especially when my mother wasn't paying attention and my brother was out of the room. Then his hands would wander under my skirt. I would feel his large palm stroking my bottom and the pressure of his fingers as they found the secret place between my legs. I wanted to tell him to stop, but without the words to express my feelings, I couldn't.

'Come here, Sally,' he would say, when I hung back from him. 'What's the matter? Don't you love your daddy?' His arms would stretch out to me as he bent down to my height. I could sense his irritation building so I would walk reluctantly into them.

With time the comforting stopped. More and more often he was annoyed with me. 'Don't be a baby – you're getting as bad as your mother,' he would exclaim, when I told him I wanted to get off his knee. My fear of his anger would keep me there while I felt the 'hard thing', for which I had no name, pressing against my buttocks.

Chapter Five

Some time between my third and fourth birthday my mother told me I was going to get a new brother or sister. I was sitting next to her on the settee, watching one of her favourite programmes, *It's A Knockout*, on the television. My mother was laughing at the contestants, who were carrying an assortment of unwieldy foam objects and trying to run over a huge inflatable obstacle course. The shapes resembled the ingredients of a hamburger. The players' aim was to deliver each component to another team member, who was waiting at the far end of the course. They would then return to the start, allowing another team member to complete the same task. Because the items were so large there were lots of false starts and falls and we laughed at their antics.

Leaning against her, I noticed her stomach had grown big and asked her why.

'It's because there's a baby inside it,' she told me. I don't remember much of the following months, just that my mother got larger and larger. Then she went away for a few days, and when she returned she was thinner and she was carrying my baby brother, Billy.

My mother was pale and tired and said she'd hardly got any sleep in the hospital. Once again, she ignored my needs, the cooking and housework.

After a week my mother's sister, my aunt Janet, came to

stay and order was restored to our home. The amassed piles of dirty clothes and bed linen were washed, dirty nappies, which had been left in an overflowing bucket in the bath, were soaked in bleach, and home-cooked meals appeared promptly on the table. She took over my bath and cream routine, got me into my nightdress and read me bedtime stories.

Our front door was forever being opened to friends and relatives who wanted to see the new baby, and every visitor who came bearing gifts cooed over tiny Billy. The sitting room was full of soft toys and hand-knitted cardigans, hats and romper suits in soft blue and white wool. A fleecy blanket that my mother had spent hours crocheting covered his cot.

'What do you think of your baby brother?' Suddenly it was the only question anyone ever asked me. Otherwise I felt ignored. Everyone's attention was focused on Billy, and even my mother seemed to have little time for me. It was the baby who was cuddled and talked to, not me.

I felt rejected and lonely, and glared at the small, gurgling addition to our family with resentment. It seemed that with his arrival it was only my father who had time for me. 'You're my special little girl,' he would say repeatedly, and I, craving attention, would cuddle up against him.

My aunt left, saying she had to get back to her own family, and once again it was my father's large hands that rubbed cream all over my body. 'I want Mummy to do it,' I protested.

'Your mother is too busy looking after the baby to put you to bed,' he said, every time I asked for her, and, taking my hand firmly, would lead me from the room.

'You're a good little girl, aren't you, Sally? You'd do anything I asked you, wouldn't you?' And when I nodded, he took his touching a stage further – he probably knew my mother was in the middle of feeding Billy. He held my small hand in his and placed it on the front of his trousers, then pushed my fingers against the fabric as he forced my hand to move up and down. Fearing that any resistance would alienate the one person to whom I was still important, I would stroke the place he directed me to. It felt hard through his trousers, and I did as instructed – I felt something twitch, as though I had woken a small living thing. My father's hot breath rasped in my ear as he moved my fingers faster and faster until I felt his knees jerk and a tremor go through his body. Then, with a sigh, he would remove his hand and push me away.

I knew I didn't like touching it, that the sensation of the 'hard thing' moving and my father's hot breath on my cheek repelled me, but I didn't know why.

Chapter Six

It was my fourth birthday. I knew that because my mother had told me so as soon as she woke me up. When she took me downstairs she pointed to a small dark blue box next to my breakfast plate. 'It's for you, Sally,' she said. 'It's your birthday present.' Opening it, I found a silver bracelet.

'Look at this! As you grow, it can be made bigger,' said my mother, and showed me how the band expanded. She placed it on my arm for me.

'You have another present,' she told me, and gestured to a huge parcel done up in gaily patterned wrapping paper and tied with gold string, which was sitting on the kitchen floor. 'Here, I'll help you,' she said, as I struggled to open it. With a few snips of her scissors the paper fell off to reveal a painted wooden dolls' house.

The front slid away and inside it had miniature wooden furniture and a family of dolls. I gasped with delight. I had seen one just like it in a toy-shop window and had pointed it out to my mother as the most beautiful thing I had ever seen. But I had never dreamt I would have one of my own.

'I made it for you myself,' my father said gruffly.

'Yes – he spent hours on it, working alone in that old shed,' my mother added proudly.

My father's arms opened and I ran into them to receive a hug. I felt the bristles on his chin rasp against my cheek before he lifted me on to his lap. 'Do you like your present?' he asked. I nodded enthusiastically. 'Well, then, give your daddy a big kiss.' I obediently pressed my lips against his cheek.

'Look, Sally, let me show you something. Do you see this tiny switch?' His finger flicked it down and tiny lights shone out of every window.

I was almost speechless with excitement as I played with the dolls' house and moved around its family of tiny inhabitants.

'Sally,' my mother said, 'go into the garden while I tidy up in here.' Reluctantly I left my adored new possession and went outside to play with my Space Hopper. Later that day my mother took me upstairs and I saw a brand new dress of pale blue cotton, embroidered with tiny pink rosebuds, lying on my bed. 'A new dress for my special birthday girl,' my mother said. 'Your nana and your cousins are coming for tea.' My hair was brushed till it shone, my face was wiped clean and the dress was pulled over my shoulders. She stood me in front of the mirror. 'See how pretty you look?' I grinned with delight at her smiling reflection.

When my nana, aunts and cousins arrived for tea they brought more gifts, and this time it was me, not Billy, who was the centre of attention. 'Happy birthday, dear Sally, happy birthday to you,' they sang, and I was hugged and kissed before parcels of all shapes and sizes were handed to me.

'Come on, Sally, you can open them,' said my mother, and before long the floor was covered with torn wrapping paper. I opened my grandmother's present first. It was a Tiny Tears baby doll, something I had dreamed of owning.

Nana showed me how I could insert a bottle filled with water into its rosebud mouth before changing its nappy when it dampened. In the other parcels I found picture books, more new clothes and last, from my unmarried aunt, a miniature tea set. 'You can have your own tea parties with your dolls,' she told me.

Pete came straight home from school to be in time for the tea. When he entered the room he thrust a small packet tied up with string into my hands. 'Happy birthday, Sally,' he said, and blushed. Inside it were some minuscule ornaments, a mirror and a set of pictures. 'For your dolls' house,' he said. 'I knew Dad was making it.'

It was his present that made me the happiest. Until now he had never taken much notice of me despite my attempts to get his attention.

I realized why I had been sent out to play in the garden that morning when my mother produced the birthday cake she had made. The white writing on top of the pink icing said, she assured me, 'Happy birthday, Sally', and in the centre there were four candles – one for each year since I had been born, I was told.

'You have to blow them out, Sally,' everyone told me in unison.

'Then make a special wish,' my mother instructed.

I puffed out my cheeks, blew hard and squeaked with delight when the flames flickered and died. But I was so excited I forgot to make a wish. I often wonder if things would have been different if I hadn't.

That evening it was my father who took me to bed. Ignoring my protests that I wanted Mummy, he led me from the room. Once in the bathroom, the same ritual followed of me being bathed, then sat naked on his knee. This time my wails at him spoiling my birthday were so loud that they brought my mother upstairs. She came into my bedroom and saw him trying to pull my pyjamas on to my small struggling body. 'What's wrong, Sally? Why are you crying?' Receiving no reply she turned to my father. 'What's wrong with her? Why's she so upset?'

'Oh, it's nothing, Laura. She slipped and fell. That's all, isn't it, Sally?'

To which, trying to stop the tears, I answered, 'Yes.' And with that one false word, my compliance had begun.

My mother stood for a moment, her eyes locked on her husband's before, seemingly satisfied with his explanation, she turned and silently left the room.

If I had been old enough to recognize the expression on her face, what would I have seen? Suspicion? Growing awareness? Or both, followed by defeat? From her actions two years later, I think it was the third.

Chapter Seven

The accident with the chip pan happened on a day that had started as one of my mother's good ones. That morning she had dressed me, brushed my hair into two bunches, then brought my colouring books into the kitchen and opened them on the table.

She put Billy in his playpen and gave him an assortment of soft toys. He gurgled away happily as he examined his pink bunny in his half-sitting position. He was just starting to become mobile so when he was in the playpen I knew my mother would be able to devote her time to me.

Wax crayons came out of a biscuit tin: she drew pictures of animals for me and I tried to copy them. 'Look, Sally,' she said, each time she drew another brightly coloured picture, and I recognized the feverish, excited tone in her voice that often came before a black day. She started to pour herself a drink from a large brown bottle, then exclaimed impatiently when she realized it was empty.

Later, with Billy in his pram, the three of us went to the shops. My mother's voice was shrill as she chatted incessantly to me and anyone else she met. As she talked her voice rose higher and higher. We stopped at the butcher to buy steak, the grocery shop where, still chattering, she bought potatoes and milk, then finally at another shop where brown bottles were passed across the counter. Even at four I felt uneasy when I saw the look of impatient pity and something bordering on contempt that crossed the shopkeepers' faces as she filled her bags and placed them at the bottom of the pram.

Once we arrived home, my mother gave Billy a bottle, then poured orange juice for me, and gulped down glass after glass of the golden liquid that came out of the brown bottles she had bought. By the time my brother came back from school her speech was slurred. He gave her a look of reproach and disappointment, then took his school books out of his satchel, spread them on the end of the table and started to do his homework.

I saw him glance anxiously at my mother's glass as she filled it again. With a sigh, he lowered his head back to his books. I sat quietly, feeling the tension that the sight of my mother drinking always brought, and watched her prepare the food for the evening meal.

'What are we having for tea?' Pete asked, when he saw her peeling potatoes.

'Steak and chips,' my mother said brightly, as she put the chip pan on the stove. Bored, I wandered over to stand next to her as smoke rose from the bubbling fat and she started to throw in the slices of potato.

'Dad will be home in a minute,' Pete warned her, when she picked up her empty glass and moved to where the brown bottle stood on the counter. She turned to reach for the bottle and her wide sleeve caught the pan's handle. My elder brother, seeing what was about to happen, leapt from his chair and pushed me as hard as he could. He was fast enough to prevent the whole pan of boiling fat falling on me but not fast enough to stop large drops splattering on to my head and arms.

I screamed in fear and pain. Pete poured cold water over me as Billy howled and my mother shrieked. It was at this moment that my father walked through the door. He took one look at the scene, assessed what had happened and scooped me up in his arms. Through my pain I heard, 'Accident – didn't see her – sleeve caught,' tumble out of my mother's mouth.

'You've been drinking again,' my father said flatly, then turned to my elder brother. 'I'm taking Sally to Casualty. Stay and look after Billy – your mother's too drunk to be trusted.' With that, he carried me to the car and drove at great speed to the hospital.

'She's had a very nasty shock, but she's going to be all right,' the nurse said, after a cursory examination.

Patches of my hair had to be cut off before my burns could be dressed. I wailed at the sight of the long blonde strands on the hospital floor almost as much as I did at the pain I was in.

'How did you manage to spill that pan, Sally?' the nurse asked, when my sobs had finally stopped. 'I'm sure your mother told you not to touch it.'

I looked at her blankly because I knew it was not me who had spilt the fat, but I didn't want to say who had.

For several weeks after the accident my mother appeared very subdued. There was no sign of the brown bottles or of her feverish activity. During that time, she seemed to have neither good days nor the ones she called her 'black days'; instead there were days I remember as grey. She was dry-eyed and apathetic. There was no flurry of activity in the kitchen, with new recipes being tried out, and the meals she gave us were bland and repetitive.

Chapter Eight

There were times when I thought I was to blame for my parents' arguments – my mother had shouted my name at my father when I was in bed.

'Why is Daddy so cross?' I asked her once, when he slammed the door after him as he left for work.

'Oh, Sally, it's not your fault, it's mine,' she replied sadly, then gave me a reassuring hug. But she didn't answer my question.

There was one row that I knew I'd caused. My mother had roused herself from the settee where she had spent the afternoon and was busying herself sorting out the evening meal. My stomach rumbled as I watched her. She had given me just toast and Marmite for lunch and I was very hungry.

'Wait till your father gets in,' she said impatiently, when I asked for a snack.

I watched as a dish of shepherd's pie went into the oven and vegetables simmered on top of the stove. Pete had his head down and was finishing his homework, ignoring me and my mother. My father was late that night, and by the time he came in the dinner had been ready for over an hour but my mother refused to give any to either my brother or me. 'For once we're going to eat together as a family,' she said crossly, when we complained, although it was her lethargy that had forced us to eat so little during the day.

I heard his footsteps on the path before she did and was hovering near my mother when the back door swung open and my father swept in, bringing with him a gust of cold air. 'Here, Sally,' he said, spreading his arms wide for me to run into. 'Look what I've got for you.' He pushed a bar of chocolate into my hand. 'Doubt your mother's cooked anything decent so have this,' he said, as he bent down, swung me up in his arms and planted kisses on my cheeks. I smiled at the sight of the blue and gold wrapped bar and forgot briefly that I didn't like him holding me. 'It'll help your burns get better,' he added, giving my mother a sour glance.

Greedily I peeled back the wrapping on my chocolate.

'David, dinner's been ready for an hour,' my mother snapped. 'It's most probably ruined by now.' Then, seeing I was about to bite into the chocolate, she said, 'Sally, leave that! Not until you've eaten. I don't want you to spoil your appetite.' To my dismay her hand stretched out and she took the chocolate from my fingers.

I felt my four-year-old face turn scarlet as it was whisked away, tears gathered in my eyes, which were suddenly bright with outrage, and I opened my mouth to let out a bellow of rage.

My father scowled as he sprang towards my mother. He caught her arm in a vice-like grip and forced her fingers open. 'Are you telling my daughter she can't have what I gave her?' he shouted into her face, which had gone white. 'Weren't so bothered a few days ago when you nearly killed her, were you?' The family dinner was forgotten as the shouting began.

My brother slammed his books closed, picked them up

and walked out of the room. 'Not hungry any more,' he muttered, as he left, but my parents hardly noticed his departure. They were too busy glaring at each other. I knew that in some way I was to blame for this but I didn't know what I'd done.

As the two people I loved went on shouting at each other, I looked from face to face and my world crumbled. My howls turned to frightened hiccups as tears slid down my cheeks. My father picked up the chocolate from the floor where it had fallen and returned it to me, but I no longer wanted it.

He knelt by my side and, in a voice that was suddenly gentle, said, 'Eat it, Sally – it's your favourite. Don't take any notice of your mother. She's always trying to spoil things.'

Confused, I looked from one adult to the other. I wanted to please my father but was scared of my mother's disapproval if I did as he said.

Seeing my reluctance, my father glowered at me. 'Don't eat it, then, you spoilt little cow.' His body shook with rage as he turned to my mother. 'Now look what you've done. Always spoiling things – you're a selfish, pathetic bitch, aren't you?'

I gulped and more tears ran down my cheeks. All of a sudden I wanted to go to the lavatory – and I wanted my mother to take me. I looked up at the two faces above me, convinced that I had somehow caused all the anger that was swirling around the house. I wanted my mother to pick me up, take me somewhere quiet and tell me that everything was going to be all right. I pulled at her skirt for attention. 'Mummy –'

'Not now, Sally,' she replied tersely.

Their anger was too much for me and my bladder opened. At the sight of the yellow puddle forming at my feet I wailed in shame and confusion.

My father looked at me with something approaching disgust and turned to my mother. 'Will you get this little cry-baby changed, for God's sake, Laura?' Wordlessly my mother took my hand and led me out of the room.

'I'm sorry, Mummy, I'm sorry,' I kept saying tearfully, and my mother knelt down, put her arms around me and kissed me.

'It's not your fault, Sally,' she said, but her flat tone did little to console or convince me that I wasn't the cause of the row.

After she had changed me and wiped my tearstained face, my mother brought me back into the kitchen. Then it was my father's turn to gather me up in his arms. He hugged me and said he was sorry he had frightened me. 'Daddy loves you,' he whispered, as he stroked my cheek.

But, even more confused, I turned away.

Chapter Nine

Several months after the birth of my brother the extremes of my mother's depression gradually returned. Once again tears continuously streaked her cheeks, her eyes and nose were always red and the smell of stale apples clung to her from quite early in the morning.

I knew from remarks I overheard on Sundays that my father's brothers and their wives held the opinion that my mother was self-indulgent or 'soft in the head', and that the unhappiness that hung over our home was considered to be of her making. All I knew was that I loved her and wanted her to smile again, and my father to stop being angry with her all the time. I didn't tell them how I felt when, night after night, I lay in bed trying to block out the sounds of his rage and her despair, which drifted through the walls of my room.

These sounds had become so commonplace that eventually I would fall asleep with them ringing in my ears. But the night my mother was rushed to hospital was different. This time my father's shouts were louder and her screams, which ricocheted off the walls and vibrated through the house, were piercing. On and on they went. I heard my mother shrieking my name, my father shouting back and her voice repeatedly screaming, 'Liar!'

Suddenly my father's shouting stopped, and the only sounds were the wails of distress from my baby brother who, woken by the noise, was crying in fright. I heard my father's footsteps on the stairs and then, apart from the hiccuping sobs of the baby, there was silence.

I fell back into a restless sleep, only to be woken again by Pete yelling frantically for my father. There was the sound of rushing feet and a voice I scarcely recognized as my father's called my mother's name over and over. A short while later I heard the back door opening and my grandmother's voice. Bewildered, I wondered why she had arrived. Somehow I knew something very bad had happened.

I slipped out of bed and, clutching my favourite doll for comfort, I opened my bedroom door and crept out. For a few seconds I hovered on the landing, then tiptoed down the stairs to the closed door of the sitting room.

My hand reached for the knob but I was too scared to turn it. Inside the room, I knew, there was something I didn't want to see. Instead I pressed my ear to the keyhole and tried to make out what my nana and my father were saying. There was fear in my grandmother's shrill tones, an emotion I had never heard from her before, and it terrified me. Still with no way of knowing what had happened unless I entered the room, I forced myself to push open the door and froze when I saw the tableau inside.

My grandmother, with a look of horror on her face, was staring at the same thing as my father and Pete were: my mother sprawled silently on the settee.

'Mummy,' I whispered, but she didn't stir. Her blonde hair partly obscured her white face but I could still see the mascara smears that had mixed with her tears.

'Sally, you shouldn't be in here. Go back to bed,' my

grandmother said, but no one moved to take me out of the room. 'Your mummy's not very well,' she continued. 'The doctor's on his way.'

'Mummy,' I wailed, wishing she would open her eyes and scold me for being out of bed, then take me back to my room – but she didn't move.

I looked around at the grim adult faces for reassurance and saw that my father's face was pale while Pete's was stained with a flush that crept from his neck and all over his face. His fists clenched and unclenched and his breathing came in short shallow gasps. His distress communicated itself to me.

Before I had time to take in any more, I heard a siren and blue lights showed through our curtains. There was a flurry of activity as my father rushed to the door and let in two men in uniform, who came into the room.

One bent over my mother, lifted her eyelids and placed two fingers on her neck and wrist. The other picked up the empty pill bottle on the table and asked questions I didn't understand. I heard my father telling them about the empty brown bottles and that she'd been depressed.

'Have to get her to the hospital now, so she can have her stomach pumped,' the one who was bending over my mother said tersely. I watched with alarm as my mother was placed on a stretcher. A blanket was tucked around her, and then they carried her out. I rushed to the front door and watched as they put her in the ambulance, and my father climbed in beside her. Then the doors were shut, the siren sounded and, with blue lights flashing, the vehicle sped off. Despite the lateness of the hour the street was full of curious neighbours, who looked at Pete and me with pity as they speculated in whispers on what had happened.

As the ambulance disappeared from view I threw myself on to the pavement and screamed. I felt my nana's arms going round me and trying to lift me but it was Pete who carried me inside and placed me on the settee where my mother had lain. They both leaned over me, making soothing sounds, and my nana told me that my mother was going to be all right. But no amount of reassurance could stop my howls of fear. It was not until I was too exhausted to cry any more that, with my grandmother's arms around me, I finally fell asleep and was carried back to my bed.

My father returned in the morning, grim-faced, pale and tired.

'Your mother's going to be all right,' he said, to Pete and me.

'Where is she?' I asked, and was told that she had to stay in hospital for a few days until she was better.

I didn't believe him. People who were taken away in ambulances didn't come back. I knew that because I had seen one of our neighbours, an old man, carried out of his house on a stretcher and he had never returned. Instead, a few days later, I had seen his wife, dressed in black and leaning on the arm of one of her sons, getting into a large car. Later, other cars had arrived filled with black-clad people. I was told the old woman had 'lost her husband' and had been at something called a 'funeral'.

My nana stayed at our house that day, and after he'd had some sleep and a meal, my father returned to the hospital.

Chapter Ten

After my father had left I started to bombard my brother with questions. But Pete just told me I was too young to understand and refused to say anything more on the matter.

It was not until I was two years older that he told me more about what had happened on that night. That evening I had been in the lounge and witnessed yet another of the frequent rows between my parents. My father had returned home from work to find my mother smelling of drink and with no dinner ready for him. Not only were the breakfast dishes still in the sink but Billy, in a dirty nappy, had been left to cry in his cot. 'What have you been doing all day, Laura?' he yelled. 'Look at this house! It's a slum! I work and work and work, and then I come home to find you just lying there and nothing to eat.'

Lost in a fog of drink and depression, she gazed blankly at him and said the day had slipped away without her noticing.

The row between them developed from there with each having a different agenda. He wanted her to see how furious he was at her neglect, and she was trying to divert his attention from the fact that she had been drinking.

'You spend money like water,' he shouted. 'Do you think it grows on trees? You just spend, spend, spend!'

'Things are expensive, these days, David,' she said.

'Drink is, you mean! Do you think I don't know what you've been doing with your housekeeping money?'

She tried to deny it but we all struggled to understand what she said because her speech was so slurred.

His anger became directed at Pete then, not just at her. 'Could you not have tidied up?' he yelled, when he saw that the sink was a swamp of dirty dishes left soaking in scummy water, and that on every surface ashtrays brimmed with cigarette stubs. 'And what about your baby brother and Sally? Could you not have looked after them either?'

'Not my job, and I've got my homework to do,' was Pete's defiant answer.

More shouting followed, and I stared at my feet, just waiting for it to finish. Eventually, once his rage was spent, my father stomped out of the house saying he was going to spend his hard-earned cash at the fish-and-chip shop. When he returned, the three of us ate in the kitchen while my mother lay silently on the settee with her face to the wall.

Pete and I, knowing that the truce would only last until the food had been consumed, disappeared to our rooms as soon as we had eaten. Neither parent came to see if I was all right and I put myself to bed without bothering to wash or clean my teeth. Once under the bedclothes I fell into a troubled sleep until my mother's screams woke me.

It was some time after that when Pete, unable to sleep and feeling guilty at having slunk off to his room, had gone to see if she was all right. Expecting a tear-sodden mother he had instead found an unconscious one. Seeing that my father didn't appear to know what to do, he had phoned my grandmother, and on her instructions, he had called the ambulance while my father had just stood helplessly by.

After her first admission to hospital, my father and his family were forced to acknowledge that my mother's behaviour was not all her fault. The doctor had told my father that she was clinically depressed and that the drinking aggravated it. Depression was an illness, he had explained, which could be controlled by medication once they found out the best type for her. He went on to say that she was in a place where she would receive the right help, so there was no reason why she should not make a full recovery.

During that time it was decided that Billy would stay at my nana's house where she and my aunt could look after him. Pete and I would remain in our home, but every morning on the way to work my father would take me to Nana's house.

My mother was kept in that special hospital for six weeks. To me, a few months short of my fifth birthday, it seemed like a lifetime and, convinced that my mother was never coming home, I was inconsolable. When she saw my gloomy little face my grandmother would try to cheer me up. 'Your mother will be home soon,' she told me reassuringly, several times a day. 'She has to rest before she'll be ready for visitors,' she would say, when I pleaded to be taken to visit her. I knew that my grandmother and my father had visited so why could I not go as well?

Eventually when my grandmother realized that until I saw my mother I was not going to believe that she was getting better, she agreed to take me to see her. She bought a posy of flowers for me to take, and put me in the blue dress my mother had given me on my birthday, with the silver bracelet I had insisted on wearing. I sat anxiously next to her on the bus. I clutched the posy so tightly that the green liquid from the stems splashed on to my dress as I stared out of the window, willing the journey to go faster.

'You have to remember that your mummy is very tired, Sally,' Nana kept telling me, but I was too excited at the thought of seeing her to pay much attention to that.

As soon as we entered the hospital my nostrils were filled with the smell that pervaded every corner: a mixture of disinfectant, cabbage, body odour and flowers; a smell that, ever since, I have associated with illness. I wanted to run and find my mother but the yards of shiny corridors and the sheer size of the building were intimidating. Instead I took my grandmother's hand and held it very tightly.

'Here we are! This is your mother's section,' she said, when we had walked to the far end of the corridor. A nurse unlocked the metal door and we entered a different area. Still holding my hand tightly, Nana led me into another corridor where we passed rooms furnished with rows of white-covered beds and an office in which several nurses were sitting. Passing them, we entered a large sitting room, painted a dull putty colour.

I saw my mother straight away: her hair was tied neatly back from her face and she was wearing one of my favourite outfits: a long denim skirt with a cream lacy jumper. She was sitting in an armchair by the window. I wanted to run to her but suddenly I felt shy.

'Come now, child,' said my grandmother, giving my hand a gentle squeeze. 'Give your mummy the flowers.'

Suddenly tongue-tied, I held them out and my mother smiled. 'Sally!' she said, as she took them from me.

I searched her face for the mother I loved. I wanted her arms to go round me and for her to hug and kiss me. I wanted to hear her tell me how much she had missed me and how she was looking forward to coming home. But instead she just took the flowers and placed them on the small table beside the chair. This woman, who looked at me with a faintly puzzled expression, was not the mother who smiled and laughed, or the one who turned from me with tears running down her cheeks. It was as though a stranger had invaded her body, leaving a woman who sat hunched in her chair just staring vacantly at us. She started a sentence but let the words tail off and looked around in a bewildered way, as if she was wondering who had uttered them.

My grandmother did something that surprised me. She took my mother's hand and spoke to her almost as though she was a child. She told her how much I had wanted to see her and how I had wanted to look pretty and bring flowers. My grandmother chattered on about the baby, how he was growing and how he had cut his first tooth.

A pretty young nurse, seeing my grandmother and me, came over, her starched uniform crackling as she walked. 'So is this your little girl, Laura?' she asked my vacant mother brightly. 'She looks just like you.' For a few seconds, there was some animation in my mother's face as she told the nurse my name and how old I was. But I

Chapter Eleven

The following Sunday, before the church service began, my grandmother took me to Sunday school. 'There will be plenty of other children there for you,' she said, as she pushed me through the door of the church hall.

The short curvaceous teacher smiled at me as she showed me where to sit and explained that she was going to read a Bible story to the class.

Over the next few Sundays I heard how Jesus had walked on water, fed a multitude of people with one loaf and a few fishes, made sick people well and saved a fallen woman. The word 'miracle' was repeated; a word that I tucked firmly into my mind.

Prayer, we were told, could help make miracles happen. When I asked my grandmother what that meant, she told me Jesus listened to every child's prayers so if we really wanted something good to happen we could ask Him at night when we prayed.

What I wished for more than anything else was my mother, the one I loved who smiled at me, to return home and my skin to be unblemished. So at night I asked Jesus to listen to my prayers. 'Everything you say in prayer travels straight up to heaven,' my grandmother had assured me. But when, the next morning, my livid patches were still there and there was no news of my mother's return, I wondered if He had heard me or, even worse, had decided to ignore my pleas.

Chapter Twelve

As the days passed, nightmares invaded my sleep and my eczema spread. The weeks that my mother was away seemed endless. Our home was so quiet without her and Billy. Pete was different too: he had ceased to do his home-work on the kitchen table; instead he went to a friend's house after school and returned home long after supper time.

My grandmother tried to keep my mind off my mother's absence and read me stories, but she couldn't do what my mother had done, making them up and putting me in the centre of the story. When she took me to the park she tired quickly when I wanted to be pushed on the swing, and at her house, she didn't watch the television pro-grammes that my mother and I had enjoyed together.

'Sally, shall we bake gingerbread men?' she would say, in an effort to put a smile on my face, but the tears would seep down my cheeks. The smell when she took them out of the oven reminded me of my mother.

Missing her became a constant ache, and every morn-ing when I woke I would for a few moments expect her to walk into my room, then remember that she wasn't at home. It was my father who got me out of bed and dressed before taking me to my grandmother's house.

'Why don't you leave her with me?' my grandmother would ask, when he delivered me each day.

'Better for her to sleep in her own bed,' was his quick reply. Every night he would bath me, rub cream on my body, then sit me naked, except for a towel, on his knee. I would hear his voice telling me that he loved me much more than Mummy did. After all, he was there with me.

'It's me who loves you most, Sally,' he kept repeating – and, confused by my mother's long absence, I started to believe him. Bewildered by what was happening to our family, I liked being held and hearing the words of love that I so missed from my mother. I would close my eyes and, half asleep, snuggle up against him as his hand gently stroked my back and shoulders.

But I didn't like what followed, when it wandered down my tummy until it went in between my legs. My body would stiffen, but he would whisper soothing shushing noises in my ear until, more relaxed, I leant against him again.

My mother had been in hospital for about a week when he kissed me, not on my cheek but on my mouth. His tongue, large and slimy, slipped between my teeth and I recoiled with distaste when I felt his saliva drip on my chin. 'That's what daddies do with special little girls they love,' he said. He took my fingers and grasped them firmly as he pushed my hand downwards. Only this time they touched something hot. I knew without looking that it was the hard thing and that he had taken it out of his trousers.

He ran my fingers up and down it and all the time I squeezed my eyes shut for I didn't want to look down and see it. 'Good girl,' he kept saying, as his arms tightened around me, 'good special girl.' And I, wanting so much to be told that I was good and therefore loved, did what he requested without protesting. He showed me what he wanted as his hand closed over mine, squeezing my fingers tight around the thing. That first time he groaned, as though in pain, and, startled, I tried to remove my hand.

'No,' he said, gripping it so hard it hurt, and moved my fingers up and down faster. He groaned loudly again, and something wet and sticky covered my hand. He hugged me then and, taking my hands, he wiped them with a flannel. 'You're my special little girl,' he told me, before pulling my nightdress over my head and putting me to bed.

Some basic instinct warned me that this was wrong but I was too young to question it or do anything about his actions. It was a nightly bathtime ritual that, gradually, step by cautious step, he had presented to me as normal. Without my mother or Pete in the house, he was free to bath me without being caught. So when he uttered the words of endearment I needed to hear, I would say the words he expected of me: 'I love you too, Daddy.'

Chapter Thirteen

It was August when my mother finally came back from the hospital. The Saturday morning she was due home I had woken as soon as the sun had risen. There were flutters of excitement in my stomach as soon as my eyes opened: this was the day I had been longing for. I lay in bed visualizing how different life at home would be now my mother was returning. She would give me my baths and put me to bed; she would play with me and read to me and tell me her wonderful stories.

A few days earlier my grandmother had told me that my mother was well enough to come home and had helped me make a big card of welcome. On it I had crayoned a yellow sun shining above a square house. I had coloured in the door and windows and then drawn a family of stick people. Circles represented their faces and, with a red crayon, I had given them all wide smiles.

My nana drew some large letters, which said, 'Welcome home, Mummy', and I coloured them in, then stuck on cut-out stars and glitter. It took pride of place in the centre of the table next to the flowers my grandmother had cut from her garden.

The house was spotlessly clean – my aunt had seen to that while my grandmother had stocked the fridge with lots of food. I waited till I heard sounds of movement, which told me Pete and my father were up, and crept down the stairs. Before we had finished breakfast my grandmother arrived with a gurgling Billy and all the paraphernalia that accompanies a baby. She had brought more food to put in the fridge and a large casserole dish of her chicken stew. 'Just needs heating up,' she said, as she placed it on top of the stove. 'She won't want to cook on her first day back.'

It was the middle of the morning when my father left to collect my mother. Pete, for once, did not leave the house, but waited impatiently with our grandmother and me in the kitchen. I could hardly contain my excitement and every time I heard a car coming I rushed to the window to look out.

'He's only been gone a few minutes, got to give him time,' my grandmother and brother kept telling me, but nothing could keep me still.

When, finally, I heard my father's car draw up I rushed to the door, flung it open and ran outside. 'Mummy, Mummy!' I shrieked, as I hurtled towards her. She looked the same as she had before she'd gone away. Her hair was loose and hung to her shoulders and she was wearing the outfit I loved, the one she'd had on when I'd visited her in hospital. 'Give me a hug, Sally,' she said, as she leant down and embraced me.

Once she was inside she went to my elder brother and I saw his arms lift and close tightly around her.

My grandmother rose from her seat. 'Good to have you back with us where you belong, Laura.' At her words, I saw my mother's eyes fill with tears. She went to where Billy sat in his playpen and leant over it to coo a special greeting just for him. He gave her a slightly puzzled look, instead of bestowing one of his wide smiles on her, and turned his head away. A look of dismay crossed my mother's face when she saw that Billy didn't appear to recognize her. When she picked him up, he cried and stretched his arms towards my grandmother.

'He'll get used to you again soon enough,' said my nana. 'Six weeks is a long while for a baby. Just give him time.'

Tea was made. My nana, as well as cooking our evening meal, had brought homemade scones and a chocolate cake, which she put on the table. I heard my mother saying how good it was to be home and how she had missed us all. But the smiles did not hide the worry that crossed my grandmother's face when she saw all the bottles of pills come out of my mother's bag to be placed on top of the fridge. 'Too high for little hands to reach,' my mother said, and added that if they were there she wouldn't forget to take them.

Chapter Fourteen

It wasn't long before I was thinking that the hospital had sent back a different mother. The tears and blank-faced depression might have vanished but so, too, had the laughing woman with the sparkling green eyes. This was not the mother I had missed so unbearably; the mother who ruffled my hair and, with her arm around my shoulders, held me against her comforting warmth when I was upset or afraid. The mother who had dressed small cuts and laughed at my chatter, baked me gingerbread men and told me exciting stories seemed completely lost to me.

She appeared much more concerned by Billy's indifference to her than anything else. His smiles were for my grandmother and, in fact, almost anyone else who came to our house, and for the first few days he appeared to ignore her. Trying to win him round she spent the mornings playing with him while I was sent out to the garden to entertain myself on my Space Hopper. 'He needs to get to know me again,' she explained, when I whined that I was bored, thirsty or hungry. 'He's punishing me for leaving him – he's too young to understand,' she added.

But I was, too, which she didn't seem to take into account. When I pleaded with her to take me to the park she said she was too tired. When I asked if we were going to the shops she said Nana or Pete would get everything we needed. I was too young to realize that my mother neither wanted to confront the neighbours nor to be lured into the shop that stocked those brown bottles. So, not understanding her motives, I felt dejected at the lack of time or interest she seemed to have for me.

More casseroles and pies arrived from my grand-mother's kitchen. 'She's not up to cooking much yet,' she said, each time she delivered one.

It was at the end of the summer when I was due to start school that her reluctance to leave the house became more apparent to me. First she told me that my grandmother was going to come to take me shopping for my uniform. I was crestfallen: I had thought my grandmother would look after Billy and I would have my mother all to myself on that special day.

I had imagined us going to the park on the way to the outfitter's. I had hoped that, just for one afternoon, her attention would be focused on me.

I was sulky when my grandmother arrived to collect me and she immediately realized it was my mother I wanted with me. 'She needs a little time to get better, Sally,' was all Nana said when I complained that my mother never wanted to do anything with me.

In the shop my grandmother put on her glasses to read the list that the school had provided. She chose a navy blue pinafore dress, two white cotton blouses and a pair of lace-up black shoes. But nothing was going to please me and, rebelliously, I decided I hated the feel of the new clothes. They were stiff and scratchy and I moaned ungratefully. My grandmother took no notice. 'They'll soften up once you wear them in,' she said, before picking up the packages and leading me out of the shop.

The following week I started school. That day my mother dressed me in my new clothes and produced a brown-leather satchel, which she told me every schoolgirl needed. My hair was brushed and I leant against her, liking the feel of her running the bristles through my hair. Then she tied it into a smooth ponytail and stood me in front of the mirror. 'Now don't you look smart?' she said.

It was not until I had swallowed my last mouthful of breakfast that she informed me Pete was taking me to school instead of her. 'I can't leave Billy,' was the excuse she gave, adding that as Pete's school adjoined mine, it made sense for me to go with him.

Tears were of no avail; neither were the protests that I didn't want to leave her. My brother dragged me out of the door and we set off. Slouching along with his hands in his pockets, Pete refused to walk slowly and I had to scuttle to keep up with him.

'Don't be such a cry-baby. You're embarrassing me,' he said impatiently, when my tears threatened to overflow. 'Don't see why I've got to take you anyhow. It's her job,' he added.

'She's not well,' I said indignantly, even though just a short time earlier I had thought the same thing.

'She's never well, is she?' But underneath his words I sensed a layer of fear – after all, she was his mother too.

The school was barely ten minutes' walk away and for the rest of that time neither of us spoke. When we arrived anxious parents were departing, small children looked tearful and the teacher in charge of the infants' class was busy keeping us all together. There were a few faces I recognized but a sea of others I didn't and I stood shyly on the edge of the group.

The teacher rescued me by telling us all we had to follow her into the classroom.

It was when we had the break that the questions started.

'What's your name?' asked one little boy, and I told him. But the next caught me unawares.

'Why didn't your mummy bring you? Mummies always do.'

As I tried to answer those questions I could feel the dreaded itching and my fingers started rubbing at my skin. Seeing me scratching, one little boy pointed to the rash which my sleeve failed to cover. 'What are those?' he asked, with a sneer.

Self-consciously I tried to tug my sleeve down to cover the rash.

'Ugh,' I heard someone else say, and I cringed with embarrassment.

'You talk funny,' said a third.

'I don't,' I said.

'You do,' jeered a fourth. 'You sound like a baby.'

'Wownd and wownd,' another mimicked – I couldn't pronounce my Rs.

I knew by the end of that day that school was not going to be a place I liked. I felt like an outsider but there was also the nagging fear that my mother might disappear again while I was away from her. Even though she was always at home waiting for me, the anxiety refused to go away.

Chapter Fifteen

I had been at school a few months when we had our first lesson on telling the time.

'Who can tell me what numbers the hands of the clock are pointing to?' the teacher asked, indicating a large cardboard clock perched on her desk.

My hand shot up in the air. This was something I knew about for my grandmother had taught me how to count to twelve and how to tell the time. Now it will be me the teacher praises, I thought – being complimented was becoming more and more important to me.

Before the teacher could utter my name I heard sniggers and gasps of pretend horror and the shrill voice of the little girl who sat next to me saying, 'Please, Miss, Sally's dripping blood everywhere.'

Looking at my arm, I saw blood had oozed through my sleeve and tiny droplets had fallen on my desk. Ashamed, I blushed.

The teacher gave an exasperated sigh and marched up to me. My classmates turned to watch as she rolled back my sleeve exposing the rash and the vivid marks where my fingers had scratched it. 'Come with me. We'll have to get that looked at that.' With my head down, I followed her to the headmistress's study. As we walked down the corridor I tried to concentrate on the sound of her shoes making a rhythmic tattoo on the wooden flooring, which had been worn smooth by the passage of time and the tread of thousands of small feet.

The headmistress looked at my arm and told my teacher to return to her class. She would, she said, bring me back in a few moments. She rubbed on some ointment, then tied a bandage firmly in place. 'Now, don't scratch it again,' she said curtly. I felt humiliated – and the treacherous tears spilt down my cheeks, while a bubble of snot dribbled from my nose. 'Blow your nose, child, and stop snivelling,' said the headmistress, handing me a tissue. Then she took me back to the classroom.

When I went in, more than twenty pairs of eyes looked curiously at me. As I went to sit down at my desk I heard, 'Don't want to catch it, Miss. Make her sit somewhere else.' It was the child who had been next to me.

'Don't want her sitting next to me, Miss, either,' said the little girl on my left.

'Nor me,' said another shrill voice, until the whole class-room was clamouring.

The teacher tried to explain that it was not my fault and that it was not contagious, but the children continued to express disbelief. In the end, finding herself no match for the determined five-year-olds, she gave in and moved me to an empty desk near her.

That was the start of my being taunted and ostracized by my peers.

Chapter Sixteen

In the playground I encountered groups of small children who sniggered when I walked past. I would hear their ringleader muttering encouragement. From behind me came the jeer that seemed to follow me everywhere, 'Dirty, spotty, scabby Sally.' I would stand on my own, trying to block out the hurtful words. When I went to the school dining room, children would slide up on the benches and make sure it was impossible for me to join them. 'Ugh, look at that, puts you off your food,' said one girl, when the rash had spread to my neck.

'Stay away from me! Don't want to catch what you've got,' said another.

One of my cousins, who was a couple of years older than I, tried to protect me: 'Leave her alone. She can't help her rash,' she told the group who were mocking me, but they just laughed before running off.

My teacher tried to intervene. She tried to explain what eczema was and told the children she didn't want to hear them ridiculing me again. For a while the taunts ceased. But one girl had eavesdropped on an adult conversation and learnt why my mother had been in hospital. After that nothing was going to stop them talking about me.

'My mum heard your mother's mad,' said one little boy, viciously. 'Heard her tell my dad so. He said she was a mad drunk – knows the man in the offie, he does.'

'Yes,' said another, not to be outdone, 'and my mum says your house is dirty.'

The insults rained down and I put my hands over my ears.

'How was school?' my mother would ask me when I arrived home and I, not wanting to see her rare smile fade, would talk about the teacher and what I had learnt that day. But she didn't ask me if I had made any new friends, and if she noticed the hollow note of bravado in my voice, she never questioned it.

Chapter Seventeen

The fear I felt that my mother might disappear again made me follow her around the house demanding constant attention. I sensed that this had begun to irritate her but, given my fears and insecurities, I was unable to stop myself doing it.

When I saw Billy being constantly picked up and cuddled I felt a dull aching jealousy. I became convinced that he stopped my mother spending time with me. I resented the fact that every visitor went straight to where he was and made cooing noises, and loathed it when they commented on how appealing he had become.

'Skin like peaches and cream,' was one compliment that was repeated regularly.

'Look at that hair,' said another, as her hand reached out to tousle it. Instead of the straight limp hair that I had, Billy's head was covered with soft blond, almost white, curls.

'With those blue eyes and that Cupid's bow mouth, he looks just like one of God's little angels,' my grandmother said, over and over again.

I didn't think he was an angel when he threw his toys out of the playpen and I was asked to pick them up, or when he disrupted our mealtimes by flicking food in the air. On the rare occasions when my mother had time to read to me or made up her magical stories, he always seemed to need attention and she would stop and rush to him, leaving the story unfinished and forgotten. Under lowered eyelids I glowered at the baby, wishing my mother had never brought him home.

'Come on, Sally,' my mother said, after a few weeks of my sullenness, which showed whenever I saw my baby brother receiving attention. 'You can help me today.'

I looked at her expectantly, wondering what she had for me to do, only to be told it was to help with Billy's bath. At least I wasn't being sent into the garden to play or being told to keep still or that I was getting under her feet.

She laid a towel on the floor and put the blue plastic baby bath on it. Once she had filled it with warm water and tested the temperature with her elbow, she added a few drops of baby oil. She took off Billy's romper suit and nappy, then lifted him into the water. Bathtime was something that Billy clearly liked. With a wide smile on his chubby little face he gurgled with glee as his chubby hands went palms down on the surface of the water. He slapped it vigorously, sending miniature waves to spill over the side.

My mother handed me a flannel. 'Wash him like this.' She showed me how to move the cloth gently across his rounded shoulders and arms. He looked into my face and laughed, and I saw that two tiny teeth had appeared.

My mother pointed to a few bumps that were showing in his gums.

'That's more teeth ready to come through,' she said.

I thought that must hurt and asked her if that was why he cried at night.

When she told me it was, I began to feel the start of something approaching sympathy for my little brother.

'Well, you and Pete cried a lot too when your first teeth were coming through,' she told me. But somehow I couldn't picture Pete ever being the same size as Billy.

When we had finished bathing him, she lifted him out and laid him on a padded plastic mat. 'You dry him,' she said, handing me a towel, and I wiped it slowly across his back and up and down his arms. All the time, with those two teeth showing in an expanse of pink gum, he smiled happily at me and I forgot my jealousy.

'Look at his baby bangles,' my mother exclaimed, laughing, as she touched the dimpled rolls of rounded pink flesh on his arms and legs. 'You had them too when you were his age.'

My mother blew noisy raspberry kisses on his plump little stomach and he waved his arms, kicked and chortled. Looking at his naked body, so round and pink, and smelling his warm baby smell of clean skin and talcum powder, I was suddenly enchanted by him. His eyes looked into mine, a dimpled hand reached out and his fingers grasped mine trustingly. With that touch all remnants of my resentment evaporated to be replaced by a wave of love, and for the first time the word 'my' came before 'baby brother'.

'Can I hold him?' I asked, when my mother had pinned on a towelling nappy and buttoned him into a clean yellow romper suit. Smiling, she propped me against her on the sofa, placed him on my knees and put her arm around my shoulders. My arms slid round him protectively.

Blue eyes stared into mine and he gave another face-splitting smile and I found myself giving him one back.

At five I did not have the words to express what I felt

but if I had I would have said things like 'perfect' and 'love'. After that I was always smiling at him and offering to help with feeding, changing and bathing him. It was my hand now that passed him his toys and it was me who rushed to his playpen to coo at him.

Chapter Eighteen

I think my mother tried desperately hard to hide her underlying sadness. She smiled when I prattled on about my daily achievements at school, cooked tasty meals and even resisted arguing with my father. But it must have been there all the same. It was just that none of us saw it.

'She's better now,' my brother said.

'She's doing so well!' my grandmother said, to anyone in the family who asked about her.

'I love you, Sally,' my father said, as he stroked the top of my thigh.

It was when, once again, I smelt the sour aroma of stale sweet apples, a smell that even toothpaste failed to camouflage, that I knew the brief period of happy days was coming to an end. With the smell came the dark depressions that even the pills were not strong enough to hold back. Once again her tears fell and my father, exasperated by what he called her 'selfish neurosis', took himself off to the pub, often returning late in the evening.

My brother ate his meals in silence, then disappeared into his room; the sound of loud rock music drifted under his door. Once again, we were having Sunday lunch at my grandmother's house and yet again Pete and I overheard the comments about our mother's many shortcomings.

On one of her dark days I had another accident. She had picked up a brown bottle only to find it empty when she tipped it against the rim of the glass. That day her desire for drink was stronger than her maternal need to look after her children. Telling me she was going out to a neighbour and that she would only be a few minutes, she ran out in the direction of the off-licence, leaving me in charge of my baby brother. Billy was sleeping peacefully when she left but the sound of the door slamming behind her woke him.

His eyes opened wide and he began to shriek when he saw she wasn't there. I tried to remember what my mother had said to do to amuse him when he was crotchety; something about 'diverting his attention'. I called his name, pulled funny faces at him, stroked his hot little head and tried to give him a fluffy toy but nothing did any good. His face went red and his mouth gaped as his high-pitched howls nearly deafened me.

In desperation I ran out of the house to find my mother. She couldn't be far away, I thought. She'd said she had to borrow something from one of the neighbours.

In the panic caused by Billy's cries I had forgotten I wasn't wearing shoes and I didn't notice the broken bottle in the gutter. Thinking that my mother might be in one of the houses opposite, I stepped off the pavement and trod on the shards of glass. A searing pain shot through me and then it was my turn to scream. Neighbours from both sides heard the commotion and came rushing out.

'Sally, whatever are you doing out in the road – and with no shoes on too?' one said, as she lifted me up.

'Where's your mother?' asked another and, receiving no answer as she called into the house, carried me bleeding and sobbing into the lounge.

She gasped when she saw Billy, who was still howling in his playpen. 'She's never gone and left them both alone?' one said to the other, as she sat me on the settee and inspected the damage to my foot. 'It's deep! It's going to need stitches,' she said, as she tried to staunch the flow of blood.

One of them ran to the house of another neighbour, whose husband worked the night shift and was at home. He was quickly woken and I was lifted into his car. One woman stayed to look after Billy and prepared to confront my mother when she returned. The other came with me to the hospital where, once again, I was treated in Casualty.

'You're becoming quite a little regular here, aren't you, Sally?' said the nurse, as she wrote some notes in my file. I remember the two women exchanging glances while the doctor stitched my foot. I screamed as three injections were administered to my bottom.

'The first will help the pain, the second is to stop infection and the third is to prevent tetanus,' he explained carefully to the neighbour. 'No school or games for you for a few days, young lady,' he said gently to me, as he stroked my head. He told the neighbour when I should come back to have the stitches out and gave her a large box of pills.

That day, there was no covering up my mother's actions. My grandmother was phoned and told not just about my accident but how Billy had also been left alone in the house.

That night there was another row between my parents, and my father shouted so loudly his face went almost purple with rage. 'Useless,' he called my mother. 'You're a useless, pathetic drunk who's not fit to be a mother.'

My grandmother, who had remained to cook our evening meal and to make sure I was settled, tried to tell him to calm down. She said that he was frightening us, but his rage was so intense that he brushed her aside. I was terrified that my mother would have to leave us again and, still in pain, I hobbled to her for protection against an anger I couldn't deal with or understand.

His face was inches from hers as he gripped her arms and shook her. 'You pull yourself together, Laura, or you can get out of this house! And don't you think you'll ever see your children again.'

Chapter Nineteen

It was after the accident, as she called it, that my mother started collecting me from school. To begin with, we went straight home but within a few weeks she was stopping at the shop that sold the brown bottles.

'Sally, you won't tell your father, will you?' she asked. I was a small child, too young to shoulder such responsibility. Terrified by what he had said about making her leave, I kept quiet even when I was questioned by my nana and my father.

She might have thought she had drawn the wool successfully over everyone's eyes but I sensed they suspected she was still drinking. I saw my father opening cupboard doors, looking behind curtains and chairs and once he even looked inside my dolls' house.

I never told him where my mother hid her drink. Not even bothering to hide from me what she was doing, she would open the brown bottles and tip the contents into empty baby formula containers. She then put the empty bottles back into their brown-paper bags and hid them under the blanket in Billy's pram. She would throw them away when she went out, but only when she had looked around and checked that no one was watching.

Each day when school finished I would race to the gates, always a bit scared that she wouldn't be there. Two months later my fears were realized when she wasn't outside to meet me. I waited and waited for her, and when I saw my nana walking towards me, I knew she had disappeared again.

I was told that my mother was very tired and that she'd had to go back to the hospital for a rest but that she would be home again in a few days. I found out later that her craving for drink had reacted badly with her drugs and this time the mixture had nearly killed her. The same neighbour who had found me in the street was alerted by Billy's wails and had knocked furiously at the door. When she got no reply, she went in and found my mother unconscious on the floor with an empty cider bottle by her side. Once again an ambulance had arrived in our street, but this time when her huddled form was carried out in broad daylight the whole neighbourhood stood watching and gossiping. 'She loves it more than us,' my brother said angrily, when he heard.

'Yes, she does love it more than you, but I love you best, Sally,' my father whispered into my ear, whenever we were alone.

Chapter Twenty

We never knew which neighbour had reported my mother's behaviour to social services, only that someone had: this time her relapse brought a social worker to our door. It was my grandmother who explained to me that a lady was coming to talk to us when Pete had returned home from school. My father was also to be present.

'She just needs to ask you both a few questions,' Nana continued. She told me I mustn't be scared and should answer truthfully. That afternoon, instead of going to her house, she brought Billy and me back to ours. He was popped into his playpen and toys were arranged around him in the hope that he would be quiet. Nana busied herself cleaning the house and plumping up the cushions, constantly glancing at her watch. I sat at the table and looked at a picture book – Nana had said it was too messy to colour in or use my paints.

Pete had also been told to be on his best behaviour. He had started on his homework when there was a knock at the door. My father went and brought in a woman who seemed about my mother's age. She was sallow-skinned with a sleek dark brown bob that fell forward over her face. She looked earnestly at all of us, and surveyed the room through rimless glasses before finally taking a seat at the table. She opened her briefcase and took out a file and a pen.

My grandmother spoke first. She told her that while my mother was away she and her unmarried daughter had charge of Billy. 'So Sally is left here?' the woman asked quickly.

'No. My son brings her over to me in the mornings and collects her when he returns from work,' Nana said.

It soon became clear that it was me she was most interested in talking to. My father said that I was too young to understand what was happening. 'That's as may be,' she said, 'but I still need to ask Sally some questions.'

To begin with she asked me the same things that adults always seem to ask small children – how old was I and what did I like most at school. Once she saw I was at ease with her, more searching questions followed. 'What do you and your mother do in your spare time?' she enquired. I told her about the books she read to me, the pictures she drew and the stories she made up just for me. She then moved on to my two accidents.

First she questioned me about the chip pan. 'How did it happen, Sally?' Bewildered, I looked at my father.

'She caught it on her sleeve, didn't you?' he said quickly and I, clutching at his explanation, replied, 'Yes.'

'Let her answer for herself,' the social worker said sternly, then turned to me. 'Is that what really happened, Sally?'

Again I mumbled, 'Yes.'

Pete said nothing, but I saw him glance at my father.

The next questions were more difficult. She asked me why I had run out of the house in bare feet and where my mother had been.

Once more I looked at my father but no help came

from him this time. I looked at the floor and mumbled that I didn't know.

'It was my fault,' Pete said unexpectedly. 'Mum had just popped over the road and I was meant to be watching the two of them but I went up to my room to get something and Sally ran out.'

The social worker gave him a penetrating stare but Pete just looked guilelessly straight back at her.

'Well, I doubt if Sally can remember much about those days anyhow. That accident with the chip pan happened some time ago,' interrupted my father, before I could be questioned about the truth of what Pete had said. I saw the social worker scribble in the file before asking me more questions.

Was I happy at my school? I replied, 'Yes.' She looked doubtful and asked me if I had made many friends. Not knowing what answer was expected of me I looked at her helplessly and confirmed what she suspected.

I started to get restless then. Somehow I knew that my answers to her questions were important. But there were too many of them and I was worried that I might say the wrong thing. All I could think was that I wanted the social worker to go.

'She's tired,' my father said. 'I think that should be enough for now.'

The social worker smiled at me and said I'd been very helpful, then gathered her things and left.

Later, after Pete had made the excuse that he needed 'to study' and had gone to a friend's house, I went to my room and was playing with my dolls' house with the door open. Voices drifted upstairs and became raised as I heard my grandmother and father having a heated argument. I crept quietly to the top of the stairs and sat down to listen to what they were saying.

'Why did you get the children to lie?' she asked him, and before he had a chance to say he hadn't, she answered for him: 'We both know what happened. She was drunk again, wasn't she?'

'And you know what would happen if that woman had been told the truth, don't you?' he retorted. 'They could say she's an unfit mother and take Sally and Billy away.'

I heard my grandmother mutter something about how it might be for the best if she wasn't allowed near us, and knew she meant my mother. 'This has to be the last time you hide things, David,' my grandmother added, before she left, taking a sleeping Billy with her.

'What did that lady want?' I asked my father, when he was getting me ready for bed.

'She wants to take you away from us,' he answered. 'It would mean you'd never see any of us again. And you wouldn't like that, would you, Sally?' I shook my head miserably.

'So if that lady comes to the school and tries to see you on your own, just say you can't talk to her unless your nana or I am there. Do you understand?'

Seeing my face pucker with worry and fear, he put his arms around me. 'But Daddy won't let anything bad happen to you.'

Still terrified at the pictures he had conjured up, I was unable to speak and stared mutely at him.

'I'd never let them do that, Sally,' he said. 'You're my

special little girl and I love you. And you love your daddy, don't you?'

'Yes,' I whispered.

'Time for your bath now,' he said, and the ritual started. His fingers took mine and placed them on the front of his trousers. 'Just move your hand up and down like this,' he whispered, as he gripped my wrist tightly and forced my fingers to move.

I wanted to climb down from his knee or wriggle out of his grasp but the fear that he was the only person who could stop me being taken away for ever, never to see my family again, kept me there, doing the thing I didn't want to do.

Chapter Twenty-one

The next morning on the way to school I realized that Pete was the one who was most upset by my mother's relapse. 'That social worker will be back if it ever happens again. Don't think we've seen the last of her,' he said morosely. 'They'll take us all away, if she's not careful. It happened to a boy in my class. They said his parents were unfit and now he's in a place he really hates.' He looked down at me. 'It's not fair, is it? It's his mum and dad's fault but he's the one who's made to pay.'

I had no answer for him. His voicing of his fears made mine even more real, and for the next few days I kept my eyes open and scanned every grown-up I encountered. I was scared I'd see that lady with her notebook coming towards me. She came in my dreams and pulled me out of my bed, and it was only when I screamed myself awake and was stroked calm by my father, that I understood she wasn't there.

A week later my mother returned. There were promises that she wouldn't leave me alone again, but I no longer believed her. I watched her surreptitiously, looking for any sign of her becoming sick again, fretting about what Pete had said. At night my fears turned into nightmares.

Tossing and turning, I started wetting my bed and woke up to a sick feeling of shame. My mother kept telling me it wasn't my fault, but still I felt it was.

'Sally, what's the matter?' my mother asked, when she caught me alone in my room silently crying.

'Pete said that if you go back to hospital again we'll all be sent away,' I managed to say. 'And I don't want to go into a home and never see any of you again,' and as I voiced my fears, more tears poured from my eyes and my voice turned into a frightened wail.

For a moment she looked shocked. 'Oh, Sally, whoever put that idea into your head? Nobody's going to take you away. I'm better now and I'm not going to leave you ever again. I love you too much for that.'

I wanted to believe her. I wanted to believe that she loved me, but in my mind I could hear the echoes of my father's voice telling me that it was he who loved me best and that she loved drink more than she loved any of us.

My eczema became worse and there were times when, busy with Billy or lost in her own world, my mother sent me to bed without bathing me and putting my cream on.

Chapter Twenty-two

There was great excitement at school when it was announced that our class was being taken to the swimming-pool. An instructor was going to teach us how to swim. Boys and girls were given separate days for the classes and I was in the one for children under eight. We walked in a straggly crocodile the few hundred yards to the pool. With the strong smell of chlorine and disinfectant in our noses, we raced into the female changing rooms. The other little girls were impatient to shed their clothes and don their swimsuits.

Rubber swimming caps were pulled on over hair and, squealing with excitement, they headed for the water. I could hear them screaming as they stepped into the small footbath that prevented you carrying germs into the water. The noise echoed around the changing room as I stood in the corner holding a tog bag with my new costume in it, hoping I could hide in there and that my absence would go unnoticed.

Underneath my school clothes I knew the rash covered most parts of my arms and chest. My mother had forgotten to put my mittens on and in the night I had scratched the itching till it bled. There were oozing sores and scabs behind my knees, in the soft creases of my elbows, on my shoulders and at the tops of my legs.

At six years old I was too young for real vanity but I

was old enough to understand mockery, and I could imagine the taunts and jeers that would come in my direction if my pitiful body was exposed to my classmates.

However, when our teacher did a head count, she knew one child was missing and came in search of me. 'What are you doing hiding away in here, Sally? You should have your swimsuit on by now,' she said impatiently. 'Come on, let's get you undressed and in the pool. Lift your arms up.' Reluctantly I did so.

I heard her gasp as she pulled my dress over my head, and wanted to disappear through the floor.

'Oh, Sally,' I heard her say, 'you poor little soul. Why didn't you say anything?' At this kindness I burst into tears and without saying any more she wrapped me in my towel and took me to the person in charge of first aid.

I heard the words 'mother' and 'neglect' being whispered between them. Something cool was put on my sores, gentle soothing words were said to me and then I was taken back to the changing room and allowed to get dressed. I watched the swimming lesson from the gallery, sitting next to the teacher, relieved I wasn't part of it.

It was the teacher who took me home and spoke to my mother. I don't know what was said but I remember it made my mother cry. She kept telling me she was sorry, she hadn't known it had got so bad.

That night, after my mother had bathed me and put on my cream, she tied my cotton mittens over my hands. After I had been tucked in, I lay in bed thinking of the next day and how I would have to face my classmates. I thought that, even though the other children had not seen me when my dress was taken off, somehow they would all know what had happened. I knew what they thought of me – that I was dirty and that my mother was crazy for they had said it so many times to my face.

It was after hearing these taunts that, when my mother wasn't looking, I started eating soap. When there was just a small piece left in the bathroom I hid it in my bedroom and ate it when nobody was about. If it cleaned the outside of me then it could clean the inside too, I rationalized.

Instead it made me sick.

Chapter Twenty-three

It was more than a year after she had been admitted to the hospital for the first time and several months after her relapse that my mother became ill. This was different, she protested, when she was accused of drinking again. 'So you say,' was my father's disbelieving response. Complaints that she ached everywhere and was tired were ignored. Looks of anger and frustration were directed towards her by my father's relatives.

There were times when I rushed in from the garden at my grandmother's house and the room went silent. I knew they had been talking about something they thought was not suitable for children's ears. This piqued my curiosity enough to make me creep quietly around the house and try to listen at closed doors. I heard my father saying he had been through enough and was not going to put up with any more, then my grandmother and aunt agreeing with him. For too long they had witnessed my mother's depression and her drinking: this was just another bout of the same problem, they said.

My father had visited the off-licence and when he was told she hadn't been there for weeks, he suspected her friends of buying drink for her. But it was not until school had broken up for the long summer holidays that we all gradually realized my mother was suffering from a different kind of illness. To begin with she just said she was tired and that whatever she ate disagreed with her. 'Just a bit of indigestion, Sally, nothing to worry about,' she told me, as she leant back on the settee the first day I was home. She asked me to watch Billy and closed her eyes for the rest of the morning.

Over the following days I heard her retching in the bathroom. The colour drained from her face, leaving a yellow-tinged pallor, and violet smudges appeared under her eyes. I watched her moving tiredly around the house, and when we went to the shops she dragged her feet instead of walking at her usual brisk pace. Her slender figure became gaunt and when I tried to lean against her she pushed me away, complaining of pain.

My father still refused to believe that she was unwell and kept on accused her of drinking. 'I've told you, Laura, what'll happen if I catch you, haven't I?'

Looking small and vulnerable, my mother was unable to summon the energy to argue with him.

'What's wrong with you now?' he would shout, when she told him she felt too ill to cook as the smell of food made her nauseous. You could see him smelling her breath but it was the smell of vomit that filled his nose, not the telltale notes of alcohol. Cupboards were pulled open as he stormed around the house searching for bottles.

He questioned Pete and me. Had she stopped at the off-licence, he asked me, and gave me a disbelieving look when I said no.

'Please just go and get some fish and chips for you and the kids,' she begged, when she had felt too ill to cook a meal.

'Have to ask my mother to bring round something

decent, seeing you're not up to doing anything,' he snapped. 'Can't live on fish and chips.'

Finally it was my grandmother who spoke up: she said that this time she thought my mother was genuinely ill.

'You'd better get yourself off to the doctor's,' my father told her, after Nana had voiced her concern. 'Get yourself sorted out, then maybe this house will go back to normal.'

It was my grandmother who rang the surgery to make the appointment and went with her.

Pete was given the job of babysitting and sat around morosely until they finally returned.

'So did they find out what's the matter with you?' my father asked.

That was when we were told that she was to be admitted to the hospital within a few days. 'Just for a small operation so they can see what's wrong with me,' my mother explained, to Pete and me, when we asked her what the doctor had said.

'Will they make you better, Mummy?' I asked as, with a sinking heart, I remembered how it felt at home each time my mother disappeared.

'Of course they will,' she answered, ruffling my hair. 'They always have, haven't they?'

It was later when my mother was putting me to bed that she told me it had been arranged for me to go and stay with her sister, my aunt Janet. 'Just for a few weeks,' she assured me, 'till I'm better.' It was only me who was to go: my baby brother was to be left with my grandmother, and Pete would stay at home with our father.

'It'll be a lovely holiday for you,' she said, but I was doubtful of that.

The following day she helped me with my packing. Three cotton dresses, underwear, shoes, a swimsuit and some jumpers went into a suitcase, with a couple of heavier pinafore dresses. It looked like I was going for weeks, not just a few days.

'You never know what you'll need with this funny weather, Sally,' she said, when she saw me looking worried at the amount of clothes being packed.

I chose some books and placed my Tiny Tears doll, which I had named Bella, on top of my case. 'I want to stay here with you, Mummy,' I said.

'You're going to have a lovely time, darling.' Something in her expression told me not to show any more reluctance at leaving her.

That night when my mother tucked me into bed she told me she had written down a special story for me to take away with me. As she read it to me I thought the heroine, who was a pretty little girl with long blonde hair and green eyes, sounded suspiciously like me.

The little girl's mother told her that there was a special place where she would be happy. It was a beautiful house where a very happy family lived and they would look after her. But first the little girl had to find the house, for it was hidden in the enchanted forest. I asked why her mother couldn't take her there, and was told that it was a journey the little girl had to make on her own.

'But,' said my mother, 'the mother could see the little girl. She watched her all the time, to make sure she was safe and that nothing bad happened to her.'

The next morning the little girl entered the forest where squirrels, foxes and rabbits all lived in harmony. They took

81

her hands and guided her through the trees and hid her from the dragon that also lived there. When night came, the trees made their leaves fall into a soft pile for her to sleep on and wrapped their branches around her to protect her. When she awoke, the squirrels brought nuts and berries for her to eat and the fox gave her leaves filled with sparkling dew to quench her thirst. Again, she set off to find the house and silently called to her mother: if she could see her, she thought, then surely she could show her the way.

There was a rustling in the undergrowth and instead of her mother a bright-eyed rabbit appeared. 'Follow me,' it said, 'and I will take you to where you want to go.' For the rest of that day it hopped along in front of her, only stopping when it came to a clump of wild strawberries. When the little girl had eaten her fill, it went on until suddenly they came to a clearing where the sun shone brightly on a beautiful castle.

'This is the place you have been searching for,' the rabbit said. 'The people who live here are waiting for you.'

The little girl asked if the rabbit was coming with her but he told her that his job was done and he had to go back into the enchanted forest.

'What happened then?' I asked my mother, my eyes wide with wonder.

'Why, Sally, she went to live with them and was happy ever after, of course,' she said.

'Where was her mummy?' I asked.

'She had to stay in the magic place. She had watched the little girl make her journey and knew she was now safe. And she was happy that the little girl would be well cared for,' my mother said softly.

'And could the little girl see her?' I asked.

'No, but she knew that her mummy was still watching her every day. I love you, Sally,' she said. 'Always remember that.'

'I love you too, Mummy.' I wound my arms around her neck before I slid under the covers.

I felt my mother pulling the bedclothes up around my shoulders and, as I drifted off to sleep, her hand gently stroked my hair.

Over the years that have passed since then, that is my one memory that has been kept shiny and bright, untarnished by time. When I was still a child, that forest with the castle of safety was a picture I could conjure up at will. In my memory my mother has stayed for ever young and I can still see her with the light from my bedside lamp on her face – a face full of love – and hear her soft voice telling me the story of the little girl.

The next morning my aunt and uncle arrived to collect me. My aunt Janet, who was two years older than my mother, had her colouring but not her slenderness, while my uncle Roy, a teacher, was a quiet sandy-haired man who looked ordinary until he smiled. Then his eyes crinkled and his face suddenly seemed that of a much younger man.

My mother had a light meal ready for them but once it was eaten they seemed anxious to be on their way. I think of that day often and believe the hasty departure was to stop an emotional goodbye. Before we left my mother gave her sister a large bunch of gladioli. 'These have always been my favourite flowers,' she said. 'When one flower on the stalk dies and you remove it, another grows at the top and takes its place.'

They hugged then and I saw moisture in my aunt's eyes and wondered why the flowers had made her sad.

Then it was time to leave and my mother bent down to kiss me. 'You be a good girl,' she said, and her arms came round me and her head rested briefly on mine. My case was placed in the boot and then I was on the back seat, looking out of the window at her as we drove away. My eyes remained fixed on her as I waved until we turned the corner and she was lost to view.

That was the last time I ever saw my mother.

Two days later she was admitted to hospital and the surgeon who opened her up saw that the cancer had spread from her stomach to her pancreas and was inoperable. She was sent home to wait for death. But she had already known her fate when she sent me away.

Chapter Twenty-four

Three hours after we had left my home we arrived at my aunt Janet's house, an old two-storey stone cottage in a small pretty Midlands town. In front of it was a garden where cushioned wooden benches stood invitingly on the neat lawn. As my uncle swung open the gate for us to walk in, I smelt the perfume of the honeysuckle and jasmine that grew around it, and further along the garden path the heady scent of pink roses filled the fragrant air. I could see shrubs, and flowerbeds that were a riot of colour; a bird table hung from an old apple tree and I peered into a fish pond in which sleek golden fish swam lazily. Near the back door, which led into the kitchen, there were pots of lavender and other plants, which I later learnt were various herbs for cooking. I thought it was the most beautiful garden I had ever seen.

I was to have my own room, my aunt told me, as she led me up a steep flight of stairs. It was next to my thirteen-year-old cousin Emily's. She placed my suitcase on the bed. 'We can unpack that later,' she said, as I gazed at the floral wallpaper. There was a single bed with a pink bedspread and on it sat a large, round shocking pink and purple soft toy. I had never seen anything like it before. It had an embroidered face with long lashes and on its head it had felt hair in a Beatles style. There were feet, but no legs, and two arms for me to hold. 'It's a gonk and it's your welcome present,' my aunt told me. My affection for my

Tiny Tears doll was immediately forgotten as I picked it up and clutched it to me.

When she took me back downstairs I gazed around in wonder. The home I was used to, with all its clutter and tired furniture, was nothing like the room I was standing in. Nor did this house resemble my grandmother's, with its small stuffy rooms and her collection of ornaments, bought on day trips to seaside towns and placed lovingly on lace squares. Everything in my aunt and uncle's house was bright and clean, like the pictures in a magazine.

Small tables were placed at each end of a long tan-coloured settee. In the centre of the room there was a low coffee-table with a few magazines lying on its smoky glass top. Prints of country scenes hung on the walls, flowering plants decorated the windowsills, and family photographs in silver frames stood on the mantelpiece and the small beige-wood sideboard.

My aunt took a tall yellow and white vase from a cup-board and arranged the gladioli my mother had given her in it, while my uncle busied himself with making a pot of tea, cutting large wedges of fruitcake and pouring orange squash for me. I watched him with interest – I had never seen such domesticity in my father.

My cousin Emily came into the room and grinned at me. She had dark hair with lightly tanned skin and she was wearing blue jeans and a white T-shirt. She started telling her parents about the lovely day she had spent at a friend's house while they had been collecting me, then turned to me. 'Hello, Sally! My, you've grown,' she said, then told me she was going to show me around the house and garden as soon as tea was over.

'Milly,' she said, 'has a little sister your age, so I'll take you over to her house tomorrow.' Milly was her best friend I learnt later. She went on to tell me she had looked out some books she had enjoyed when she was my age. 'I've already put them in your room,' she added.

Faced with Emily's friendliness, my nervousness at being with relatives I had only seen until now a couple of times a year evaporated, and I began to think I might enjoy my holiday after all.

'Sally,' my aunt said, a couple of hours later, 'what's your favourite meal? I'm getting supper ready.'

'Cheese on toast,' I answered promptly.

She told me she'd had something more substantial in mind but as this was my first night I could have it. 'As long as you eat some fruit afterwards.'

That night my aunt supervised my bath and looked at the rash thoughtfully. 'You know, Sally, there are some new creams on the market now,' she told me, studying the cream my mother had packed. 'I think they would help more than this one.'

The next day she took me to the clinic where she worked as a nurse. My rash was inspected, a new cream prescribed and each night she smoothed it into my skin. She gave me fresh fruit every morning at breakfast time and told me I had to eat more vegetables and fruit: if I did, my eczema would start to get better.

Later she took me shopping and bought me some new shoes and a dress. 'Early birthday presents,' she told me when, pink with pleasure, I stammered my thanks.

When we returned to her house there was another surprise waiting for me. A gleaming black bicycle was standing outside the back door. My uncle had collected it that afternoon while we were out. 'I thought you'd like this. It's got trainer wheels for while you learn to ride it, Sally, but as soon as you can, I'll take them off,' he said, when I stared at it in amazement. 'Your aunt and Emily go cycling most weekends and I'm sure you'll want to go with them.'

It was Emily who gave me my cycling lessons, and after a few days I could ride it. Once the small wheels were removed I triumphantly rode up and down the road outside their house.

That weekend we headed out to the countryside. Emily's friend Milly and her little sister Charlene, whom everyone called Charlie, joined us and we all went cycling along the country lanes. My legs pedalled furiously to keep up but they would stop to wait for me if I fell behind.

My aunt suggested we stop around lunchtime when I was beginning to feel tired and hungry. Wheeling our bikes, we went down a path to a riverbank. There were groups of people sitting under trees with picnics, cars parked on a gravel strip and more cyclists kept arriving. 'Picnic time,' she said, but I couldn't see anything to eat.

That was when my uncle drove up and took a large wicker hamper from the car. The older girls and my aunt helped carry rugs and cushions from the boot. They opened cold bottles of lemonade and laid out cheese, hard-boiled eggs, chicken drumsticks and apples on thick paper plates.

'I did it while you were all out getting hot,' my uncle told me. 'He does this every time we go cycling,' Emily said, with a grin. That was the day when I started to see how normal families lived. I watched my uncle Roy talk to his daughter and joke with Milly and Charlie, and knew that he had never made his daughter touch and hold that hard thing. I saw how he helped his wife with unpacking and packing the hamper and how at ease all three girls were with him.

I felt a lump in my throat and tears pricked my eyes when I remembered what it had been like in our home: my father's impatience with my mother, her tears, his lack of sympathy, and how he made me touch him when we were alone.

I wished that my mother could come here so we could all live happily together, for while I missed her dreadfully I didn't miss the rows and tension that polluted our home.

Chapter Twenty-five

When she saw that my eczema was responding well to the new cream, my aunt decided the next thing to tackle was my speech. She enrolled me with a private speech therapist and explained that I had a speech impediment, which needed correcting. '"Wownd and wownd the wugged wocks the wagged wascal wan,"' was all I could manage at first, but over the weeks that, too, began to improve.

The days sped past and each one made me feel more content as I settled into the family's routine. Weekdays were spent practising my speech, reading, visiting friends with Emily and exploring the neighbourhood. We had our evening meal together before we were allowed to watch one hour of television or play with toys. Every weekend when my aunt was free from work, she planned different things for us all to do.

One Saturday she decided to take us to Birmingham's famous Bull Ring Shopping Centre. We set off after breakfast and drove down a motorway that, as we entered the city, tangled with three others. Supported by immense pillars hundreds of feet above the ground, strips of roads, on which cars and trucks moved nearly bumper to bumper, twisted above, below and around each other. 'It's called Spaghetti Junction,' my aunt said, as I craned my neck to look. 'It's just opened – and it also means we're nearly there.'

After we had parked the car in one of the many car parks, we entered the grey building where, on a wall, a huge mural of a bull informed us we were at the right place. Staring up above me I saw brightly lit floors full of restaurants and shops connected by something I had never seen before: a bank of glass and silver staircases that rose and fell of their own accord.

'They're called escalators,' my cousin said, so I stepped on and rode up and up. Exhilarated at being able to look down and see everything around me, I wanted to keep riding. We wandered around, looked in shop windows and went to the cinema where we watched *The Adventures of Robin Hood*, the latest Walt Disney film. Afterwards we sat in a café where we ate ice cream out of tall glasses and drank cold fizzy drinks. Then it was time to return to my aunt's house.

That evening my aunt got out writing paper and envelopes and laid them on the table. 'I'll help you write a letter to your mother,' she said – she wrote it and I drew pictures. Between us we told her about the bicycle rides and what I had seen at the Bull Ring. Then I wrote lots of love and drew a row of kisses.

Letters came back from Mummy, telling me she was missing me but was very happy I was enjoying myself. She drew pictures of fairies with pale wings and a blonde-haired girl in little woodland scenes at the end of each letter.

Gradually the summer was drawing to an end and I knew that, soon, a new school year would start. 'When am I going home?' I asked my aunt.

'Sally,' she replied, 'you have to stay here a little longer. Your mother still needs to rest. I've arranged for you to go to a lovely school here.'

Before I could question her any more she told me that we were going shopping. I needed nice new school clothes. We had to go into Birmingham to buy them, and I forgot my questions at the thought of more rides on the escalators in the Bull Ring.

We bought a dark grey pinafore dress, white cotton blouses, a grey blazer, a woollen jumper, regulation underwear, a gym outfit and a pair of lace-up shoes.

'You look so pretty and grown-up,' my aunt said, when I had tried on everything. In the mirror the girl looking back at me seemed very different from the one who had arrived in the Midlands just over a month earlier. My eczema was nearly gone, my hair was drawn back from my face into a long neat plait and my tanned face glowed with health. My aunt took me for lunch and ordered a hamburger and a milkshake for me. It was then I summoned up the courage to ask her the question that was worrying me.

'How long am I going to stay with you?' I blurted out. Although I was happy with my aunt and her family, I still missed my mother terribly, especially when we were buying the school uniform.

'Just until your mother feels better,' she answered, then, in an attempt to divert my attention, she asked me what I wanted for dessert.

I might have not turned seven yet but I sensed her unwillingness to answer any more questions.

A few days later my aunt took me to my new school.

Unlike my brother, who had disappeared the moment we walked through the gates, she held my hand and introduced me to the teacher who was in charge of my class. I was seated between Charlie and a red-haired girl whose freckly face broke into a wide smile when she saw me. 'My big sister is in the same class as your cousin,' she told me.

For the first time I had someone who stood beside me in the playground and invited me to visit her at her house. 'It's my birthday next week,' she said. 'You'll come to my party, won't you? I'd love you to come.'

Suddenly I had friends, little girls who said my hair was pretty and who held a rope for me to skip over during break. After one class where we had to draw pictures, Charlie and my new friend Katy said mine was the best. By the end of the day the fluttery feeling of apprehension that had been in my stomach when I'd thought of starting at a new school had disappeared.

No one talked about me behind my back or teased me about my looks. My skin and speech had improved so much I was like every other child there – but when I came out of the gate to see my aunt waiting for me, I realized again how much I was missing my mother.

Chapter Twenty-six

As autumn and its warm, golden days drew to an end, the sky darkened, with birds migrating to warmer climates, and the early-morning frost made the grass stiff and white. Christmas was fast approaching and still there was no talk of me returning home. Every time I asked how my mother was and when I was going to see her, I was told she needed to rest and the subject was skilfully changed.

Each week I wrote long letters telling her about my new friends and what I had learnt at school, and by return she sent me hers, but they seemed shorter now, there were fewer drawings and the writing was spidery.

It was when our class was rehearsing for the annual nativity play that the headmistress walked into the room and beckoned me. My aunt was coming to fetch me and I should gather my things, she told me. With a child's unclouded instinct I knew that something had happened to my mother.

When my aunt arrived I noticed that, apart from two red spots high on her cheekbones, her face was pale and drawn. She took me back to her house and all the way there I wanted to bombard her with questions but fear of her replies silenced me.

It was when we were sitting together on the sofa that my aunt took my hand and faced the heartbreaking task of telling a frightened child who was not yet seven that the mother she loved was dead.

'Dead' was a word I refused to understand; 'gone away' was something I could cope with and that was the expression I clung to.

'But where is she?' I kept asking.

'She's in heaven, Sally,' my aunt kept telling me.

'When will she come back?' I asked, and my aunt was left struggling to explain that she wouldn't. With each word she uttered I felt my head pound and my heart thump as what she told me began to sink in.

As though to comfort me, the memory of the story my mother had told me the night before I left came into my mind. 'Can she still see me?' I asked urgently. 'From heaven, can she see me?'

For a brief moment my aunt looked puzzled, then her arms tightened around me. 'Yes, darling, of course she can. She'll be there watching you for ever.' She told me how much my mother had loved me and, even though she had gone, she wanted me to be happy. She did not tell me about the months of pain my mother had endured. Nor did she say how my mother had shrunk to four stone and that even the bed sheets spread gently over her caused excruciating pain as the cancer tore away at her emaciated body. Neither did she tell me how, despite the morphine, my mother had begged God to let her die.

It was my brother who told me these things, but not until many years later. He had been there whenever he could and bunked off school to be at home with her. Finally, when she was dying in the hospital, he had held her bony hand and dripped water on to her parched lips when she could no longer sip from a glass.

He also told me she had known she was dying when

she sent me to my aunt. She had told him I needed a mother and her sister had a home she wanted me to stay in to be cared for and loved. But that day I knew none of that. I only knew that I was a very sad little girl who was never going to see her mother again.

My aunt told me then that my father was insisting he wanted me to go home and they were taking me back in a few days. I thought of a home where there was no mother and shrank back against the settee. A thick fog of misery engulfed me. When my aunt tried to talk to me and hold me, I turned away.

That night sleep would not come. I heard Emily going to bed and later my aunt and uncle too. My door was opened and my aunt whispered to me, asking if I was awake.

I held my breath and pretended to be asleep because I didn't want to talk.

In the darkness I listened to the creaking sounds of the old house settling down as though it, too, was ready for rest, but my mind refused to be still. The place I had once called home seemed remote. It was when I was drifting into that stage between consciousness and sleep that the image of the house came into my mind and, half dreaming, I saw myself entering it. My mother was somewhere inside, but instead of opening the kitchen door I climbed the stairs. I peered through the door of the room that had been my bedroom and saw it was cold and bare. I passed Pete's room with its 'keep out' sign on the door and his teenage mess inside.

Finally, as I had done so often when my mother had had a 'bad day', I peeped into my parents' room, looking for her. There was the bed with the crocheted throw I had watched my mother make, and a silky scarf was tossed carelessly over a chair, but the room was empty.

I found her downstairs. Her green eyes sparkled, a smile was on her lips, but as I moved towards her, willing her to speak, her image faded to be replaced by one of my father. Tall and handsome, he opened his arms and stretched them out for me to run into. It was his voice I heard echoing in my head.

'Sally, don't you love your Daddy? Because I love you,' and I opened my eyes with a start.

I knew I didn't want to go home.

'Can't I stay here with you, Aunt Janet?' I pleaded in the morning.

'No, Sally. He's your daddy and he misses you.'

If only I had told her then about my father and the things he made me do – how different my life would have been. I would have grown up in a loving home where his acts would merely have become a stain on my memory; one that in time I would have pushed deep into the recesses of my mind.

Later, when I reached school-leaving age, I would have talked to career advisers and my teachers and trained for work I would have been happy in. Having known caring family love I would have looked for it in the man I would choose to marry. But my silence over the next few days ensured that, for more than three decades, this would not be my fate.

A few days later, my aunt and uncle returned me to a house that, without my mother, was no longer a home.

Chapter Twenty-seven

I arrived to find a cold, distant father and an older brother who, in the few months since I had been sent away, had become grim-faced and aloof. Billy, still only a toddler, sat big-eyed and mute with a look of bafflement on his face as he watched us. Too young to understand what had happened, he was old enough to feel bewilderment and unhappiness at the permanent absence of his mother. The first few days after I had returned he stared at me as though he no longer knew who I was. He no longer played with his toys; instead he hurled them around the room. Fractious with confusion, this once happy little boy screamed in misery and anger at his mother's disappearance.

When I tried putting my arm around him his small body was sticky and hot. Needing comfort, I tried to draw it from him by burying my face in his damp hair. But it was not my thin child's arms that he wanted; his face crumpled and he let out bellows so loud it was almost impossible to believe that they could come from one so small.

But if he missed his mother I felt I missed her even more, and every time my father's back was turned I searched the house for traces of her. I stood in the bedroom she had shared with my father and remembered the times I had found her lying there with the covers drawn up over her face. The pillows on her side of the bed had been removed and his were placed firmly in the centre, which was no longer covered with the crocheted spread she had taken so long to make; it had been replaced with a drab brown blanket. Wanting to touch something that had been hers I had opened the wardrobe but it was only to find that her long floaty skirts and brightly coloured tops and scarves had all disappeared. Only my father's shirts, jackets and suits hung there.

The dressing-table was bare of her makeup and little pieces of jewellery. Not even her silver-backed hairbrush remained.

In the sitting room there were pale marks on the walls where photographs had been removed, and on the mantelpiece where my parents' wedding photographs had stood, there was a square wooden clock. Where were the scrapbooks in which she had written those stories just for me, her watercolour paintings that she had hung in the kitchen, the pictures of dogs, cats and horses she had stuck on the fridge? The house was empty of her.

At first I refused to believe that my mother was never coming back and I hated the changes in the house that seemed to deny her very existence.

'Where has she gone to?' I asked Pete, on one of the rare times he was home.

Unexpectedly he sat down beside me on the sofa and put his arm around my shoulders. 'She's dead, Sally. You know what that is, don't you? There was a funeral. They buried her, and she's not coming back, ever.' And suddenly grief poured off him in waves and I felt his chest heave and his tears as they fell. He gave deep, noisy sobs and hid his face in his hands. When finally he lifted it, I saw he was no longer a surly teenager but an unhappy lost boy with red-rimmed eyes.

'But where is everything?' I wailed.

He rubbed the sleeve of his jumper across his face before he spoke again. 'Our bloody father threw everything out,' he answered bitterly. 'He said he didn't want to look at it. He took all her clothes to the charity shop. I can't even pass it in case I see them.' Miserably he kept shaking his head as he talked, almost in disbelief. 'He took away all her things so that even the smell of her had gone. You know that smell? The one from before she was ill? I tried to find something that still had it, so I could remember it for ever. One day I got into her wardrobe and shut the door. Even though nothing of hers was there any more, you could still get a tiny hint of her. I will never forget her, and nor must you, Sally. But he won't even talk about her. It's as though she was never here. I hate him.' He wept then, and the tears ran down his face. Silently he wiped his eyes with the back of his hand, only for them to fill and overflow again as, lost in his own deep sorrow, he appeared to have forgotten I was there.

It was me then who comforted and held my big brother, and it was our shared grief that for the first time made me feel truly close to him.

Chapter Twenty-eight

The next day I went back to my old school. The children left me alone and peered out of the corners of their eyes at me curiously. Not only had I gone away for a whole term but they all knew my mother was dead. Maybe they imagined what it would be like to wake up one morning and find their own mother had disappeared. Perhaps it was just too uncomfortable for them. Too young to feel pity, an adult emotion, the children felt fear instead. They must have been told not to tease or bully me so instead they averted their eyes when I walked past them and ignored me.

At playtime it was the teacher I stood next to and she was concerned and protective of me when she realized that, no matter what was said, the children were not going to ask me to join in their games. I ached and longed for my mother every morning when I awoke and, for a few seconds, expected to hear her voice telling me it was time to get up before the realization of her permanent absence hit me. I dressed myself and went down for breakfast, which Pete now made for me. My brother and I walked to school together each morning but few words passed between us, and with every step we took my mind was full of memories of my mother.

My father, too, had changed. He seemed angry and told me that he didn't want me talking about my mother all the time. 'It was God's will to take her,' he said self-righteously.

Vainly I looked for the father who had said I was his special little girl. Not only was my mother no longer there but the father who had told me he loved me had also disappeared. In front of my grandparents or well-meaning visitors he seemed the same, but when they vanished so did his loving-father act.

It was I then who sought him out. I wanted to hear him tell me I was special and I wanted him to fill the void my mother had left. I was a small child and unaware of the game he was playing; the game to make me feel it was him I needed. Day by day he fed my insecurities by withdrawing his affection and making me doubt my mother's love for me.

'Your mother drank to escape from us all,' my father told me, when I asked why she had died. 'It proves how little she loved you, doesn't it? Because if she'd loved you she wouldn't have done it, and you would still have a mummy.'

He also told me something else that really frightened me. He said the social workers wanted to put Billy and me in a home – so I must be very good and look happy when they visited. 'And whose fault is that?' he asked. 'Why, your mother's, of course. If she hadn't cried all the time, got drunk and gone into that hospital, they would never have come here checking up on us. Just you remember that, Sally.'

Those were the last words he spoke about her, and for a long time I believed him. Maybe he was right, I thought, as, for the first time since my return, he put his arms around me and held me close. Forgetting the horrid things he had made me do before I had gone to my aunt's, I snuggled up to him. It seemed he was all I had left in a world that had become so unhappy. My grandmother did her best, but nothing could fill the emptiness my mother had left.

Within a few weeks of my return my grandmother had started babysitting on Friday nights. 'Your father works so hard,' she said proudly, 'and he needs to get out.'

The first time she was to arrive after I had gone to bed. 'Time for you to have your bath, Sally,' my father told me, and although it was earlier than normal, I went obediently upstairs. At nearly seven I considered I was old enough to wash myself. I was in the bath when, without any warning, he walked in.

'You're growing up, Sally,' he said, 'becoming quite the little lady.'

I had reached the age when I had become shy at being looked at and tried to cover the parts of me that I thought private with my flannel.

He laughed at my efforts and prised it from my fingers. 'What's the matter, Sally? You love your daddy, don't you?'

'Yes,' I whispered.

'And you want me to love you too, don't you?'

'Yes,' I whispered again, unable to look at him.

He bent down and ran a finger over my body. 'Well, then, you'll be a good girl and do what I ask, won't you?'

And for the third time I whispered, 'Yes.'

He lifted me out of the water, and I tensed as I remembered what had happened before. His hands ran up and down my damp body. 'Stand still,' he said, as I reached for the towel. Again his hand ran up my legs – and stopped when he heard the back door opening and my grandmother calling out to him.

His hand dropped from my body and, quickly wrapping the towel around my shoulders, he told me to get my nightdress on and go to bed. 'I'll see you later,' he said, as he bent his head for me to kiss his cheek.

It was my grandmother who came upstairs to me and read me a story before tucking me into bed. Clutching my gonk, I drifted off to sleep.

It was the sound of her voice saying goodbye to my father as she left that woke me. I heard him moving about downstairs and then there was the sound of the stairs creaking as he came up. Fluttering tendrils of apprehension crawled up my spine when I heard his footsteps stop outside my room. My neck prickled with fear and my stomach clenched. I closed my eyes tightly: if I was asleep, wouldn't he go away? He didn't. 'Sally, are you awake?' he asked, in a voice that sounded different: it was thicker and slurred, and the tone frightened me.

Without waiting for an answer he lifted the bedclothes and the bed sagged with his weight as he climbed in beside me. 'You're going to be a good girl, Sally, aren't you?' he said. Before I could wriggle away from him he flipped me over on to my stomach and the pressure of the pillow against my face muffled any cries of protest that I could make. He pushed up my nightdress and, as he had done earlier, stroked my bare flesh. A finger slid between my legs and stroked the soft place there. Then the hard thing rubbed against me. I tried to cry out, tried to say, 'No, don't,' and 'Please stop, Daddy,' but the pressure of his hand against my neck pushed my face harder against the pillow and silenced me.

'Lie still, I won't hurt you,' he told me. His knee forced my legs apart, one hand went under my body, raising it so my bottom was high in the air, and then he pushed the hard thing between my splayed legs. In and out of them it went, and up and down he rubbed. He was careful not to let it enter me as he rubbed it in and out of the gap between the top of my legs. I tried to struggle but his grip was too strong and my arms were powerless.

His body shuddered above me and I felt wet, sticky liquid spurting over my legs and bottom. He gave a groan of pleasure. Then, lying beside me on his back, he turned me over to face him. I opened my mouth to cry out and his hand came over it.

'I thought you were going to be a good little girl,' he muttered, but I couldn't answer him. 'I do this because I love you, Sally. That's what love is,' he whispered in my ear.

That was when I started to be afraid and, seeing it, he tried to reassure me that what he had done was normal. 'It's what daddies do with their little girls,' he explained. 'Every little girl does it. But it's a secret and you mustn't talk about it. It means you love me and you are my own special little girl. You want me to love you, don't you?'

I was too shocked and too young to reason with him and never thought to ask why, if every little girl did it, I must never talk about it. Confused by the way he had frightened me and by the warmth of his voice, I remained silent.

'Night, night. Go to sleep now, Sally,' he said, as he kissed my cheek, before climbing out of my bed and going to his own bedroom.

I listened to make sure he wasn't coming back, and when I heard his contented snores, I crawled under the bedclothes and, as my mother had done, pulled them over my head.

I cried silently; tears for the lost innocence of my childhood.

Chapter Twenty-nine

Lying in bed night after night I dreaded my father's return. Sleep eluded me and the pictures of what he had forced me to do flickered like a television newsreel behind my tightly shut eyelids. The sounds he had made rang constantly in my ears and my bedclothes still seemed to carry his smell.

I tried to conjure up a mental picture of my mother to replace those thoughts, but however much I tried there was nothing; just a blank space where once her image had been. I whispered her name over and over to myself until the word was just a meaningless sound. I no longer knew what she'd looked or she'd smelt like. Even the memory of her voice when she told me stories or laughed had disappeared. No matter how hard I tried, I couldn't find her at all.

That was what my brother had meant when he had said she was dead, I thought. Dead means that she was gone not only from the house but from my head too.

I tried to talk to Pete about it when we walked to school but the emotion he had shown when I had first arrived home was now well hidden behind an impassive mask.

In the end, finding no solace anywhere, I went to my nana with my fears. I cried and cried as I told her that I couldn't remember what my mother looked like. 'She said she could see me always,' I told my grandmother, between sobs.

'What do you mean, Sally?' she asked.

'She told me she was going to a special place where she could see me, so why can't I see her?'

It took me several attempts to tell the story that my mother had told me the night before I had left to go to my aunt.

My grandmother tried to tell me that it was just a story, but I refused to listen. 'Aunt Janet said it too!' I protested indignantly, and my grandmother, faced with my choking sobs and my seven-year-old logic, decided that if I was ever going to accept my mother's death I had to see her grave.

She took me the following Saturday. We walked hand in hand into the almost deserted graveyard. My first impression of it was how very quiet it was. The thick foliage of old trees hung over the dry stone walls and seemed to deaden the sounds of the busy traffic, and the few people who were walking among the graves seemed to speak in muted voices.

My grandmother tried to tell me some of the history of the cemetery, as she pointed to old gravestones with their inscriptions that time had faded or worn almost smooth. She told me the first ones we passed were hundreds of years old and that generations of local families lay there. We walked on moss-covered paths that led us through the graves, but however much she talked to me, the size of the cemetery with its pale headstones, almost like loose teeth in an old man's mouth, unnerved me, and I clutched her hand even more tightly.

My mother's grave was at the far end of the cemetery. Too soon for the headstone to have been erected, it was just a recently dug mound with fresh flowers arranged in a vase that was positioned where later her headstone would be. 'Your father will have it put up when the soil has settled,' she said, when I asked why there wasn't one.

'She's here, Sally,' she tried to explain, 'but it's only her body that lies here. Her spirit is in heaven.'

But I was too young to understand what she was telling me. Surely heaven was a beautiful place above the sky? Hadn't I seen pictures of it at Sunday school? In the ones I had seen there was a kind-faced old man with a long white beard and a gold halo circling his head. At his feet were golden curly-haired angels who, with heads tilted upwards, were looking adoringly at him. That's what heaven was like: a place where no one was unhappy, animals lived in harmony. It was awash with a warm yellow light. It wasn't this cold, silent graveyard full of unseen dead people.

Seeing my puzzled look, my grandmother tried again to explain that my mother's spirit was in heaven and that, yes, it was exactly as I imagined it and that, yes, my mother could see me. But it was a concept that I couldn't comprehend.

After we had left the cemetery, Nana took me back to her house. Somehow she had picked up from my questions that I thought my mother had died because she had drunk too much, and that I had started to think that it might even be my fault she had died, that perhaps she hadn't loved me enough to stay.

Knowing it was really important for me to understand

that my mother's death hadn't been self-inflicted, she tried to explain the illness she had died of. She sat me down in her kitchen, poured me a glass of milk and took my hands so she had my full attention.

'Sally, your mother did have her problems,' she said, 'but she loved you and your brothers very much. I know she drank and, as young as you are now, you know that too. But, Sally, it wasn't the drink or the depressions that killed her. It was a terrible sickness called cancer.'

Seeing that I needed more, she finally said, 'Come, I'm going to show you something. I was keeping it for you and Pete. I thought I would show it to you when you were a little older but I think you need to see it now.'

And then she handed me my mother's photograph albums. 'I took them from the house when your father said he wanted to get rid of them and I've kept them safe for all of you. They're very important for you all to see,' she said. I somehow knew that for her to confess that she had gone against her son's wishes was difficult for her.

My grandmother left me alone at the table with the albums in front of me. Opening the bright purple cover of the first and turning its thick pages, I found my mother again.

At the beginning there were photographs of her when she had been very young, almost as young as me, but even those early photos were unmistakably of her. There was one of her in a swimsuit lying on a beach and smiling into the camera, and others of her and my aunt Janet, looking carefree eating candy floss. I wondered who had taken the pictures.

I flicked quickly over the pages that included pictures of my father. They showed my parents standing together, his hand resting on her shoulder while she gazed up at him with a smile of love and happiness on her face. These made me sad because it seemed to be a look just for him, which I had never seen before. I came to one of her standing in a park. She was wearing trousers that finished just below her knees with a sleeveless shirt and by her side was a little boy I recognized as Pete.

As I turned the pages I came to a photo where I was still a toddler holding her hand, and another that I remembered Pete had taken of us when we had all gone to the park together. It was during his school holidays and just before Billy was born. That day she had packed sandwiches and drinks and we had lazed in the sunlight all afternoon.

One by one I touched them as though, if I tried hard enough, she would walk out of the pictures. And as my fingers traced her features, those lost images of her were again imprinted on my mind. I knew that, without them, my mother's face would fade completely from my memory, as it had the night before when I'd looked for her and there was a blank space. The one I liked most and just sat gazing at was of my mother standing alone. She was wearing a wide-skirted summer dress and one hand stretched up to hold her windswept hair off her face. It was in black and white but her blonde hair showed clearly. I could see that her skin glowed with health, her mouth was smiling and slightly open, showing even white teeth.

'Can I have this one?' I asked my grandmother, when she came into the room.

'Let me keep it here for you, Sally, nice and safe,' she said, 'so when you want to come and look at them, they'll all be here for you. You can come and look at them any time, Sally. You know that your mother will always live on in your and Pete's memories, don't you? She'll always be a very special part of you.'

And for the first time that day I had some understanding of what she meant and, too choked with the emotion that looking through the album had raised in me, I just nodded.

I didn't notice then that she hadn't mentioned her son at any stage.

'I have all their wedding photographs as well,' she added. But those held no interest for me.

'Have you got her scrapbooks?' I asked, thinking of the hours my mother and I had spent together sticking in the little drawings she had done just for me and the sheets of paper where she had written her stories.

'No,' she said. I didn't ask her what my father had done with them. Instinctively I didn't want to know.

'Sally,' my grandmother said, as she took me home, 'if you want to talk about your mother you must come and talk to me. Your father's not ready to talk about her yet.'

I didn't tell her that the only words my father ever uttered about my mother were too painful for me to want to hear.

Chapter Thirty

Our house was a cold, unhappy place. Pete spent as much time as he was allowed to at his friends' homes, and for six evenings a week I was almost ignored by my father.

From every Saturday morning through to the following Friday he didn't come into my room either to say good-night or to touch me in the ways I hated so much. I felt almost as though I was being punished by him for the acts he forced upon me.

I walked to school with Pete and in the afternoons went to my grandmother's house until my father came and picked me up. He said nothing to me about what had happened that Friday night after my grandmother had gone. He just cooked my evening meal and then allowed me to have a bath and put myself to bed.

On Sundays the routine never changed: it was always Sunday school, followed by church and then lunch at my nana's. On Saturdays I played on my own in the garden during the day and in the evening my grandmother brought over our groceries and supervised my bath. After that was done, my clean clothes, which she had washed and ironed, were laid out ready for me to wear at Sunday school. Before she tucked me into bed she listened to my prayers, then read me a short Bible story.

I dreaded those Friday nights. Pete often stayed at a friend's house and my father had soon got into a routine of regularly going out. The fear of his return made me burrow my head under my blankets every time I heard my grandmother leaving and the front door shutting behind her. I would start to pray that this time my father would go to his own room, but he never did. However many times I pretended to be asleep, however much I tried to huddle under the bedclothes and however many times I protested, I would feel the bulk of his body as he crawled in beside me. My nose would be filled with the fumes of beer and sweat and when he left I ached from him prodding me.

In those early days he took care not to penetrate me, but he hurt me all the same.

It was on one of those evenings that he returned home with a puppy. That Friday night my grandmother had delivered me back to the house. 'Come along, Sally, stop dawdling! Your father's been held up at work,' she said, when I asked why he hadn't picked me up himself. And, thinking my dismal expression reflected disappointment at his absence, she hurriedly reassured me. 'Don't worry, dear, he'll be back for supper. And I'll be staying with you as usual this evening – it's the weekend, you know.'

Once we had arrived at our house, my grandmother busied herself with getting the supper ready. 'Some home-made soup and your favourite meal, cheese on toast,' she told me cheerfully.

I heard the sound of his car coming to a halt, then footsteps on the path and finally the front door opened. Instead of the cold, distant father I had grown to expect, in walked the one I remembered from when my mother was alive: the father who wore the smile I had thought was just for me. 'Here, Sally,' he said, as he walked into the kit-chen, 'see what your daddy has for you,' and, poking out of his jacket, I saw a small white head.

I gasped as he unbuttoned his jacket and I saw that the little head belonged to a tiny puppy. 'Here, take her, she's yours.' A ball of wriggling fluff was placed in my out-stretched arms. I saw a shiny black button of a nose, a pair of bright brown eyes looking up at me and then felt a warm wet tongue as, seeming to recognize me as her new owner, she licked my cheek enthusiastically. With the ma-ternal feeling that very young children have towards puppies and kittens, I cradled her protectively in my arms. 'She's for me?' I asked incredulously.

My father laughed. 'Yes, Sally, she's all yours. Your grandmother and I thought you might need something to look after,' he added, still with that warm Daddy smile on his face. 'She's a miniature poodle,' he told me, 'and as she's yours, you even get to name her.'

'She's beautiful.' I was almost overcome with joy that this darling little creature belonged to me alone. At that moment I forgot everything that had happened and saw once again the father I had loved. The corners of my grandmother's mouth turned up and, seeing her face crin-kling with pleasure at my delight, I realized she had known full well why he was going to be late home.

As soon as the little dog wriggled out of my arms, Nana fussed over her, getting out food bowls and puppy food, which, unbeknown to me, she had brought with her. One was filled with water and the other with small biscuits and tinned meat. 'This will be your job from now on, Sally,' she said. 'She needs a feed three times a day until she's bigger. And once she's had her injections and can go out further than the garden, it's you who will have to take her for her walks. Your daddy's too busy to walk and house-train her.'

Newspaper was duly spread out and I was given the task of taking her into the garden to encourage her to go to the toilet there instead of inside.

After we had all had supper my father looked at his watch and said that he was going out in a few minutes. 'Come here, Sally,' he said. 'You'll be asleep when I get home.' Picking up the puppy I went to stand in front of him.

His arm went around me and he pulled me towards him. 'Come and sit on my knee,' he said, still in the old voice of the caring father. 'Not too big for that now, are you?'

And, still overcome by my present, which I held lovingly in my arms, I did.

'Aren't you going to give your daddy a kiss?' he asked.

'Yes, Sally, say thank you to your father,' said my grand-mother.

Dutifully I puckered my lips and kissed his cheek.

'What are you going to call her?'

I thought of the times my mother and I had watched a pretty blonde country and western singer and how my mother had hummed along to all her songs when she played the cassette or heard her on the radio. 'Dolly,' I replied.

My father's hand gently stroked my bare knees and his fingers ran slowly around the tops of my white knee-length socks. 'Well, she'll keep you out of mischief, won't she?' he said, and my grandmother smiled happily at what she thought she saw – a father and daughter who loved each other.

'Dolly's my present to you for being such a good little girl,' he whispered in my ear. He smiled at me then, a flickering secret smile, and it was as though the present of the puppy had somehow drawn me deeper into colluding with him and ensured that our shared secret would remain one.

That night I made her a bed with an old blanket and she curled up against me as my arm held her tightly, dreading the time when my father would come home.

I woke to the sound of him tiptoeing into my room and felt the comforting warmth of Dolly's little body being removed. He placed her and the blanket on the floor where, even at only a few weeks old, she knew to stay.

Then I felt the heaviness of him climbing into bed.

'Time for you to thank your daddy properly, Sally,' he said, as his hand slid up my legs and his saliva dampened my chin as he forced his big tongue between my tightly shut lips.

When at last I heard his satisfied grunts and felt his tensed body go slack, he climbed out of my bed and stood beside it. His voice turned into a daddy's one when he said good night and then left the room. That night my tears soaked Dolly's fur when I picked her up and placed her beside me. Her little tongue tried to catch them as they ran down my face, but there were too many for her to deal with.

Chapter Thirty-one

The Monday after he had returned home with Dolly, my father told me that the lady from social services was going to pay us another visit.

'You know what she wants, don't you, Sally?' he asked. Before I could reply he repeated the threat that, even though I had heard it three times before without anything happening, still had the power to terrify me.

'She still wants to take you and Billy away and put you both in a home. And you know what that means, don't you?'

I just stared blankly at him as the old feeling of panic took hold of me.

'I told you before what would happen if she did that, Sally. You haven't forgotten, have you? It means that you'd never see your nana, Pete or me again. And they don't allow you to have pets either, so you'd also have to say goodbye to Dolly. You wouldn't like that, would you?'

In just those few days since I had been given her, I'd come to love the little dog and the thought of losing her was unbearable. I picked her up and held her against me. 'No, they can't! Please, Daddy, don't let them,' I whispered.

'Well, as long as you tell them you're happy at home and that you're never left alone. And mind that's all you say. Do you understand me, Sally?'

I understood. I knew he meant I mustn't talk about the secret.

'So you're going to be a good girl, aren't you, Sally? And keep doing everything your nana and I ask you to?' he asked urgently.

'Yes,' I replied, looking into Dolly's adoring upturned face.

Pete came into the room then and nothing more was said to me. My brother was told that we were having another visit from the social worker and that he was also expected to be at home when she came.

'She won't want to talk to you much. You're leaving school soon anyway, but it looks good if she sees we're still a family.'

Pete just said a surly, 'All right,' then told me it was time to leave for class.

All that day at school I worried about the impending visit. A home where orphans were put, I believed, because my father had described it to me over and over again, was a huge cold place with rows of narrow beds and a stern-faced matron. Children were not allowed to play or talk and had to work before and after school, scrubbing floors and doing other chores. They never saw their families again. When they were old enough to work they were sent away to be servants in big houses and they slept in a cold, draughty attic. And I was half an orphan, after all, wasn't I?

That evening was similar to the last time the social worker had visited. My grandmother arrived at the house with a neat and tidy Billy and me, while Pete returned dutifully from school and placed his books on the table. The social worker chatted to me about Dolly. She said she could see how much I loved her and, without thinking, I told her enthusiastically about how it was my job to feed her and let her outside. Then, remembering that my father had said that if I was taken into a home I wouldn't be able to keep her, I became quiet and eyed the social worker with suspicion.

She asked me how I was getting on at school. She probed as to what I liked doing most and what I did in the evenings, how often I saw my grandmother and how much time Billy and I spent with her. But her main concern was whether I was ever left in the house alone.

I told her I was happy at school, that I liked going to my nana's house and that, no, nothing was troubling me; I told her just what my father had instructed me to say.

I heard him go on to say that his mother and sister looked after the baby full-time now and that I stayed at Nana's house until he returned from work.

The social worker left after an hour. As she gathered up her things she told me she was pleased to see me looking so well. She added that this was her last visit because she wouldn't need to see me again unless anything else untoward happened.

'You did good, Sally,' my father said, after she had gone.

I didn't know then that what I feared most was going to happen anyway. That in a year's time I would be torn away from everything that was familiar and that, once again, my life would change for the worse.

Chapter Thirty-two

Without the fear that the social worker would remove me from my home, my father thought of another ploy to intimidate the child of seven I was then. Once again he knew this would ensure my silence. He told me about heaven and how, if I was good all through my life, one day I would go there and meet my mother again.

'What did you learn at Sunday school this morning?' he asked me pleasantly, on the afternoon that he put his plan into action.

Surprised and pleased by his interest, I told him about one of the stories the teacher had read to us.

'And has your teacher told you about heaven and that only good people go there?' he enquired.

'Yes,' I replied, although I was still uncertain how we got there.

'You know that's where your mother is, don't you?'

'Yes, Daddy.'

'Now, your grandmother told you how one day when you're a lot older you'll meet her again, didn't she?'

I remembered that my grandmother had told me about heaven and how my mother would live on in my memories, but not that I would meet her again. Seeing my puzzled look, he explained that when we died all the good people went to heaven. I had been taught that at Sunday school hadn't I? he asked. I told him I had.

'Now do you know what being good means?'

I thought desperately about any misdemeanours I had committed and could think of none.

Without waiting for an answer my father carried on talking. 'It means obeying the Ten Commandments. You've learnt about them at Sunday school, haven't you?'

Anxious to please him, I warily said, 'Yes,' again.

'Name some of them to me,' he ordered, and my mind went blank.

I told him I knew the ones about not lying or stealing but that was all I could remember.

'Look here,' he said, and he opened his Bible at a pre-marked page. 'See what this says, Sally.' He read it out to me in a slow, booming voice, a bit like the minister's when he gave his sermon each Sunday. '"Honour thy father and mother."' Then, dramatically, he closed the Bible with a triumphant snap. 'That means, Sally, that you must do everything you are told to by me. If you don't, when you die you will go straight to hell.'

I didn't know what that meant either but I had heard the word in one of the church sermons and knew it was not a place anyone would want to go. My father made sure that I was fully aware of how terrible it was there. He told me about the devil and the fire and how the spirits that were sent there spent eternity in pain and torment.

'And if you were sent there because you had been bad,' he continued, seemingly oblivious to the tears of fright that were leaking from my saucer-sized eyes as he drew those pictures in my mind, 'then you will never meet your mother again. Now do you understand why you must obey the commandment?'

I burst into tears then as the thoughts he had placed in my head were just too horrific for me to cope with. But long after I had stopped sobbing they took root and stayed in my mind for a very long time; thoughts that would ensure my silence until I believed that it was too late for me to speak out about what he had done.

I had forgotten that when my mother had taken the pills he had said she had committed a mortal sin and told her she would rot in hell for ever for doing it.

Chapter Thirty-three

My life had now taken on a set pattern: school, church and walking Dolly. The last was the only one of those I enjoyed doing. Wearing her red collar and matching lead, the little white dog pranced at my side, and whenever I stopped she cocked her head upwards looking questioningly at me.

I passed boys the same age as Pete who, dressed in tight jeans that flared from the knees, their hair long and greasy, lounged around smoking on street corners and studiously ignored us. But the girls, with their minute miniskirts revealing pale legs dimpled with the residue of puppy fat, balanced precariously on platform shoes, turned to admire Dolly whenever we walked by. Their faces, smothered in thickly applied makeup to disguise their youth, always broke into wide smiles at the sight of my fluffy little dog.

'She's so gorgeous! What's her name?' they would ask and, forgetting their desire to look sophisticated, would bend down to pet her. Proud of the attention Dolly received, I took great delight in telling them.

After his confusing conversation with me about heaven, my father paid me little attention and continued to act as though the now regular visits to my room at night never happened.

Frightened both by the thought that the social worker might come back and take me away and that my father would be coming to my room the next time Pete stayed at his friend's, my sleep was disturbed by frequent night-mares. I dreamt about a huge rambling old house where white-clad children, like so many ghosts, drifted wraith-like around its empty dark rooms. These figures called silently to me and came up to me and stared into my face, but when I looked at them there was only a blank black circle where their faces should have been. At other times I was falling and I felt my body plummeting helplessly to-wards unknown horrors, the air rushing past me, as the ground came closer and closer. I would awake with a start, drenched in sweat. With my heart pounding, I was too afraid to go back to sleep in case I had to return to the dream to confront the creatures. I would search the dark-ness, frightened that something might be lurking in the corners, but then, pulling Dolly closer for comfort, I would finally fall back into a troubled sleep.

My grandmother, seeing the signs of those disturbed nights in the dark shadows beneath my eyes, asked me if anything was troubling me. But my terror of the social worker, coupled with my new fear that God saw and heard everything, ensured my silence.

On weekend nights I always went to bed very reluc-tantly and even suggested to Nana that I should stay at her house rather than her coming to babysit. But late at night, when I heard the front door open and him bid her farewell, the sinking feeling in my stomach was replaced by nausea and fear. As I listened to him coming up the stairs my palms would grow damp and I would clutch Dolly to me. She always picked up on my fear and seemed to know that she would be roughly thrown off the bed as soon as he came in. Instead of snuggling closer to me, as she always did when I awoke from a nightmare, she would wriggle free and retreat to her wicker basket on the landing before he reached the room.

It was fairly soon after my father had told me about heaven and hell that I had my first attack of asthma. It happened at school on a Thursday afternoon when my thoughts were full of dread as to what the next day might bring.

It was a spelling lesson and the night before I had painstakingly learnt the ten words that had been set for homework. But even though I was convinced I had memorized them correctly, I was equally convinced when I sat in the classroom that I had forgotten how to spell them. One after another my classmates' hands shot up in the air when the spelling of a word was asked for, and each time the right letters were given, they earned words of praise from the teacher. I just sat at my desk with my eyes downcast, nervously hoping that she wouldn't notice that my hand had not gone up once. What if she asked me to spell one of the remaining words? What if I had forgotten how to?

Suddenly there was a pressure in my chest. It was as though a thick rubber band was being drawn tight and squeezing it tighter and tighter. My throat felt as though it was closing and I coughed and coughed trying to dislodge whatever was causing that feeling. But only dry harsh barks came out of my mouth and the pressure increased. Panicked, I looked at the teacher for help and opened my mouth to speak, but could only make dry, wheezing sounds that filled my ears with their desperation.

I knew that the other children were turning around in their seats and staring at me, but I was too frightened by what was happening to care. Through my fear I heard the impatient voice of the teacher: 'Sally, what do you think you're doing?' she asked, but I could only stare imploringly at her. 'Stop holding your breath, child!' But I couldn't.

My hands flew to my neck, my chest heaved and my forehead dampened with beads of moisture. There was a rush of footsteps as the teacher's look of irritation changed to one of worry when she saw that I was frantically struggling for air. 'Go and get the teacher in the next classroom,' I heard her say to one of the children, and knew by her tone that she was frightened too.

More running footsteps and then the authoritative voice of the headmistress penetrated my panic. 'She's having an asthma attack! Can't you see her lips are turning blue?' Other words like 'ambulance' and 'hospital' floated around me.

An arm went around my shoulders and a paper bag was held over my mouth and nose. 'Try breathing into this, Sally – it will help.' Still I struggled. Black dots danced in front of my eyes and, terrified, I grasped her hand tightly.

I heard the muttering of my classmates' voices as they were ushered out of the room. Then there was just the sound of my wheezing and the headmistress's voice, trying to calm me. She kept talking slowly, explained that I was having an asthma attack and to keep trying to breathe into the bag; that an ambulance was on its way, that I was going to be all right and she was coming to the hospital with me. 'Mr Peterson,' she said – he was one of the teachers – , 'has gone with his car to get your grandmother and he's going to take her directly to the hospital so she will be there almost as soon as you are.' At that I felt a little reassured.

The ambulance seemed to take a long time to come, but in actual fact it was probably only a few minutes before, siren shrieking, it drew up at the school. Then a man's voice was telling me that they were going to put a mask over my nose and mouth, that I was not to be frightened of it as there was air inside, which would help me breathe. 'It's just your chest muscles tightening. I know it's very frightening but the mask will help you get oxygen. I know you can't speak, Sally, but just try and nod if you understand me.' Comforted by his voice I did as he asked. The mask was placed over my face and almost immediately I felt the relief as pure air reached my constricted lungs.

I was picked up, gently placed on a stretcher and covered with a blanket. Then I heard the same man telling me that I was going for a short journey. The stretcher was lifted and the next thing I knew I was being placed in the ambulance. My headmistress climbed in and held my hand as we sped off.

The panic I had experienced took its toll and I was barely conscious when the stretcher was wheeled into the casualty department. There was a needle prick and a cool hand brushing my hair off my face when I was lifted from the stretcher on to a bed and the mask was returned to cover my face. The headmistress, no longer the stern woman I knew, was still holding my hand and talked soothingly to me, assuring me that my grandmother was on her way.

When a worried Nana bustled into the ward she was accompanied by the ward sister, who had explained the situation. I saw the concern on her face that, despite her attempt at a smile, she couldn't hide. 'Well, you certainly gave everyone a scare, Sally,' she said, as she leant over me. 'But you're going to be all right now.' I felt both nauseous and sleepy when the sister removed the mask from my face. I smiled weakly at Nana but really just wanted to shut my eyes, curl up and sleep and for everyone to leave me alone.

'The sister says you're going to stay here just for a night, Sally, to make sure you're all right, and then I'll come and fetch you and take you home,' my grandmother told me, before my eyes fluttered shut and I drifted off.

Later, after I had been woken up by a nurse bringing me a tray of food, a doctor came to see me. He asked me how I was feeling and put his fingers on my wrist to take my pulse. Then he placed his stethoscope against my chest to listen to my lungs and heartbeat. 'I know an asthma attack like that is frightening, Sally,' he said, 'but the nurse will show you what to do if it happens again. It's nothing to worry about.'

I heard the nurse quietly tell him that my mother had died recently.

'Poor little thing,' the doctor said. 'No wonder she's developed asthma.'

My grandmother also mentioned the eczema that, although much better since my aunt had got me new medication, still plagued me on occasions. 'Well, children who are prone to that often also develop asthma. Many grow out of them when they reach adulthood,' he told her.

The next day it was the nurse I had seen when I came in who sat on the end of my bed and showed me how to use an inhaler. 'It was an asthma attack that you had, Sally. Do you know what that is?' I had heard the word so many times over the last twenty-four hours but I still didn't really know what it meant.

Seeing from my face that I didn't understand what had happened to me, she explained as simply as possible: 'Sometimes it can happen if you're worried about something or if the weather is damp. Your chest muscles tighten and you can't suck enough air in to breathe properly. So, was anything especially troubling you yesterday?'

'I was worried about the spelling test,' I admitted.

She laughed. 'Well, try not to in future – you don't want to have an attack every time you get something wrong at school, do you?' She showed me how to place the inhaler between my lips and breathe in as I pressed it. 'Just a couple of good puffs, Sally,' she told me. 'You have to be careful with how much you use it,' she explained, 'so until you're a little bit older your school will have one and so will your father and your grandmother. We want to make sure you know how to use it before you have your own.'

She was not to know that by handing over the power of when the inhaler could be used she had placed another weapon in my father's arsenal; one more that, over the years, he would use mercilessly. Sports, gym and all team games at school ceased. At breaks and playtimes I had to stay in the classroom.

'She's delicate! Hope she's not taking after her mother,' I heard my unmarried aunt say.

My brother diligently walked me to school each morning and my nana started collecting me from school again and made me walk straight home. Playing with other children came to an end as the family tried to protect me from anything that would lead to another attack.

There were discussions on what had brought it on but my father seemed to give no thought to those weekend nights. Neither did anyone think to put out their cigarettes when they were near me. And, of course, no one knew of the fear that had become my constant companion.

Chapter Thirty-four

At seven I remained extremely confused about my feelings for my father. In my head he became two entirely different men: one I still loved and one I feared. There was the old father with twinkling eyes and the smile I had thought was just for me; I seldom saw that man, and he was the one I missed. Then there was the nasty father who, especially since my mother's death, I wished would disappear. He was the one who was angry with me most of the time and on Friday nights came to my room and did things to me that I hated.

When we were alone, whether it was during the daytime or in the evenings when Pete was out or in his room, he avoided my eyes, and if I spoke to him he answered briefly, if at all.

'What do you want now?' was his standard reply to my trying to get his attention. What I wanted was to feel loved. But that was something I found impossible to put into words. I would search his face for some sign of warmth, some small hint that he cared for me. I needed just a glimmer of hope that he still loved me.

'What are you looking at, Sally?' he would ask, when he felt my gaze on him. Those words were, I knew, a rebuke, not a question. Sometimes he would lower the paper he was reading and look at me over the top. 'What's going on in that head of yours? Having dirty thoughts, are you?'

and when I shook my head, embarrassed, he would give a short mirthless laugh. 'I don't believe you. I can see it in those cat eyes of yours. You look just like your mother.' Then he would resume reading.

I wanted to talk about my mother, but apart from using her name to admonish me, he never mentioned her. On a few occasions, when I had forgotten that he didn't want to hear her name and talked about her, he had lashed out at me.

'Daddy says I look like Mummy,' I said to my grandmother.

Thinking that my father had paid me a compliment, she looked pleased. 'Well, you have her hair and eyes.'

'He doesn't like it. It makes him cross,' I told her, hoping to gain some understanding of why he had changed towards me, but where her son was concerned my grandmother was blind to any faults.

My grandmother sighed. 'No, Sally, it just makes him sad. He misses her.'

But I didn't believe her. If he missed her, he would have kept her pictures. If he had loved her, he would still love me, I thought sadly.

Chapter Thirty-five

Within just a few months of my mother's death my grand-mother started babysitting on Saturdays as well as Fridays. On the Saturday nights my father often stayed out and didn't return until it was time to leave for church.

'Where's he off to, then?' asked Pete, when he saw my father had left the house carrying a small holdall.

'None of your business,' said my grandmother, but not unkindly. 'He has to have friends. He needs to have a life outside the house and you children, you know.'

Pete said nothing more to her but I could tell he was angry about my father's regular weekend outings.

'He's seeing someone, Sally, I know it,' he said one morning, when we were walking to school. 'I bet he was seeing her even when Mum was alive.'

'What makes you think so?' I asked. I didn't want to think of my father being with a woman who wasn't my mother.

'Well, that was what some of their rows were about. They weren't just about her drinking, you know. I heard her saying he had come home stinking of another woman's perfume. So where do you think he disappears to on a Saturday night when Nana sleeps over?'

I waited for him to tell me more and, irritated by my silence, he moodily kicked at a stone.

'Anyhow, have you seen how he gets all dressed up like

the dog's dinner? He wouldn't do that just to go to the pub with his mates, now, would he? He splashes on enough of that new aftershave too. Naw, I know he's seeing someone, all right.'

I wondered then if the things he did with me he also did with the mystery woman. He had told me it was what men did to girls they loved. The thought of that made me feel uneasy, too.

'Pete says Daddy has a girlfriend,' I told my grand-mother.

'Well, Sally, whether he has or hasn't, that's grown-up business,' was her reply. But I noticed she didn't say it was untrue. I watched him more closely on those Saturday nights. I noticed he had bought a new suit and that a whiff of aftershave remained in the room even after he had left it. I knew from looking in the bathroom that his shaving kit and toothbrush had disappeared and guessed they were packed into his holdall. And I knew that my brother was right: he didn't come back on those nights.

And I wondered what she was like.

Chapter Thirty-six

Nearly a year after my mother had died my father sat Pete and me down and told us he was planning to remarry and that he was bringing his fiancée home to meet us.

Pete went pale as he stared at my father in complete disbelief. 'No way!' he yelled. 'I'm not living in this house if you bring her back here. We haven't even put the headstone up on Mum's grave yet and you're talking about bringing another woman here to replace her.'

'Sally and Billy need a mother,' my father retorted, paying no attention to the anger and pain on his elder son's face.

Pete glared at him, and the room was thick with the open hostility that hovered between them. 'And you couldn't wait, could you?' Pete spat. 'So, who is she, anyhow?'

My father tried to tell him with a mixture of justifications and protests that he had met her where he worked. That she was the daughter of his boss – and 'No,' he replied, to Pete's furious accusations, he had never taken her out when our mother was still alive.

'So how old is she, then? Your boss is only a bit older than you!' he said, with something approaching a sneer.

'Not that it's any of your business, she's twenty-four,' my father replied defiantly.

Pete snorted. 'Twenty-four! Well, I don't need a new

mum who's only seven years older than me! Anyhow, I'm leaving here – I've got a job lined up, so don't include me in any of your pathetic arrangements.' And, with that parting shot, he bolted from the room and I heard the back door slam as he left the house.

'You'll like her, Sally, she's nice,' he said to me, 'and you'd like a new mummy, wouldn't you?'

But I still missed the mother I had lost a year earlier and, unable to think of a suitable reply, I looked at him dolefully trying to understand the true meaning of his words and Pete's response. What did he mean, 'a new mummy'? 'I don't know,' I replied.

'Well, you're going to get one, and that's that,' was all he said.

A week later he told us we were going to meet her because he was bringing her to the house for tea. 'Her name is Sue,' he added. 'Auntie Sue to you, Sally. I want you to be nice to her.' He flashed me one of his old smiles.

'Count me out,' Pete told him firmly and within seconds another of their rows erupted.

On the Friday before the Saturday that Sue was expected at the house my father didn't come home for the first time. 'I'm staying at yours until Sunday,' my grandmother told me, when I arrived at her house after school. 'Your father's staying away this evening,' she informed Pete, when she arrived with me, Billy in his pushchair and a bag containing an assortment of groceries.

Pete announced that he had no intention of being in the house when 'that Sue' arrived and that Nana needn't bother making him any supper either. Loftily he explained to Nana that he had made arrangements to spend the whole weekend with a friend. Then, picking up his duffel bag, he left. Somehow I sensed that he blamed my grandmother as well as my father for this new woman coming into our lives.

That night, despite the atmosphere that Pete had created before he left, I went to bed feeling much happier than I usually did on a Friday. Nana was there and my father wasn't coming home. My darling Dolly was curled up beside me and I wondered if a new mummy would keep my father away from me on Fridays. I hoped and prayed so.

That Saturday morning my grandmother moved from room to room, making sure that our house was clean and tidy. She dusted the furniture, wiped the bathroom and kitchen surfaces with bleach, and wonderful smells of home baking came out of the kitchen.

In the early afternoon a freshly washed Billy was dressed in his newest outfit and he sat on the floor surrounded by toys as Nana made every effort to keep him clean and quiet. She had already selected a clean dress for me to wear and, once I had walked Dolly, I was bathed and changed too. I was told to stay indoors so, like Billy, I couldn't get dirty.

I was sitting on the sofa, trying to read a book, when I heard my father's voice as he walked towards the front door. Then it opened and I saw Sue for the very first time. I stared at her in astonishment for she didn't look like anyone I had seen on our estate. Tall and slim, she was dressed in a pale pink trouser suit that flared over her high-heeled silver platform shoes. Her dark auburn hair was cut in a long shaggy bob and her face was perfectly made up. I stared at her and watched as her eyes, which I later saw were a light grey, peered around the room through very long and thickly mascaraed lashes. Her gaze fell on me, and her mouth, which was painted a pale pearly pink, stretched into a smile. 'Hallo,' she said. 'You must be Sally. Your daddy's told me lots about you and I just know we're going to be friends.' One of her hands with their long silver nails dipped into the large carrier bag she was holding and came out with an oblong box. 'I've brought you a present.'

Opening it, I found a flaxen-haired Barbie doll inside. I forced myself to return her smile as I pretended it was something I wanted more than anything else in the world. But I felt a small lump of disappointment. Since Dolly's arrival, dolls had become less and less interesting. Even my Tiny Tears one, Bella, spent most of her time lying neglected in my toy cupboard. That year I had also learnt to read and had discovered what fun there was to be had inside the pages of books. I would have preferred a new one, rather than this doll.

'What do you say to your auntie Sue, Sally?' said my grandmother, more to establish that I was to prefix Sue's name with that sign of respect than to tell me that a 'thank you' was expected.

'And who's this little man?' Sue cooed, as she turned her attention to Billy, who, with his freshly combed blond curls and clean rosy cheeks, was looking like a deliciously rounded cherub. A soft toy was handed to him. His podgy little fingers curled round it and his face broke into a wide smile that showed his little teeth.

'Oh, isn't he just so adorable? You could eat him up!' exclaimed Sue, looking excitedly at both my grandmother and father. I noticed that she made no effort to touch my little brother.

Dolly, used to getting attention from everyone who came to our house, looked at her expectantly, waiting for the customary pat. Receiving a dismissive glance, she slunk over to sit by my side.

My grandmother, much to my annoyance, fussed around Sue, ignoring Billy and me. I pulled Dolly on to my lap to pet her and reassure her that she was loved.

Tea was poured into the best china cups that had been a wedding present to my father and mother. Golden scones still warm from the oven were piled on a plate and placed on the table, along with a coffee and walnut cake my grandmother had baked that morning. Plus there was a selection of sandwiches – ham and tomato, salmon and cucumber, and egg mayonnaise, which, the crusts trimmed off, had been cut into neat triangles.

Leaving Dolly on the sofa, I took my place next to my grandmother.

'Haven't you forgotten something, Sally dear?' asked Sue.

I had no idea what she was talking about and my mind raced as I tried to think what it could be.

Seeing she had not just my attention but my father's and grandmother's, she gave one of the high-pitched tinkling laughs that by the end of the afternoon I would have grown to dislike.

'Your hands, dear! You haven't washed them after stroking that dog, have you?' I looked to my grandmother for support. Surely she wouldn't allow Sue to usurp her like that.

Instead of supporting me, my grandmother agreed with the comment. 'Sally, do what your auntie Sue tells you,' she said firmly. With that sentence my grandmother made it clear that, however short a time Sue had been in my father's life, she was now going to be in control of mine.

Sue seemed content in her small victory and then proceeded to pick at a sandwich and half a scone but shook her head adamantly at a slice of cake. 'A girl's got to watch her figure,' she said, patting her flat stomach. Her laugh rang out again when my grandmother and my father told her she was perfect as she was. More tea was poured and something approaching conversation was made. I realized then that this was not the first time Nana had met Sue and I felt a sudden spurt of resentment. Why had it taken so long for us to hear about her? Why had my grandmother not told us? I felt a sense of betrayal then, and whatever my grandmother had said since my mother had died, I wondered if she had really liked her. Round and round those thoughts went in my head, and I looked at the intruder with suspicion.

'I think your daddy looks just like Harrison Ford, don't you, Sally?' Sue asked, when she caught me looking at her. I had heard older girls refer to the *Star Wars* actor as a 'dish' and squirmed with embarrassment.

The moment the tea was finished, Sue made it clear that it was time to leave. One slim hand covered my father's. 'David, we don't want to be late, do we?' Apparently they had arranged to meet another couple. 'We've got to drive back to my neck of the woods and it takes for ever,' she said, by way of explanation to no one in particular. A quick visit paid to our bathroom, or 'the little girls' room', as she called it, fresh pink lipstick artfully applied, then goodbyes were hastily said. A quick hug for me, a pat on the head for Billy, a smile for me from my father, and they were gone, leaving a waft of Sue's overpowering perfume clinging to the room.

I stood there with a lump in my throat. In just that short visit I had seen the reality of the situation that she was now the most important person in my father's life and, because of that, my grandmother would always take her side over mine. Her presence took away the last of my security and I knew that day that any changes she would bring were not going to be for the better, as far as I was concerned.

After that visit two things changed. As good as his word, Pete left school and moved out. He had a job, he told us, and didn't want to stay where the woman he believed had been the cause of his mother's unhappiness was welcome.

'It's not true what Pete thinks,' my grandmother tried to tell me, but I believed my brother.

The second change was that my father started staying away in the week as well as at weekends, but seldom on a Friday night. I learnt later that on those nights Sue had what she called her 'catch-up' time with her girlfriends and had refused to give it up.

If I had hoped that her presence in my father's life was going to change how he was towards me, I was soon proved very wrong. Not only did he come regularly to my room but now that Pete was gone he no longer had to creep furtively between the two bedrooms. Also, what made things even worse was that I never knew now which night he was going to choose. Every time I heard him on the stairs I feigned sleep, praying that this would be the night he would leave me alone.

In the daytime, in front of other people, he always appeared to be a caring father, but when we were on our own he alternated between being distant and leering at me.

'Just you and me left in the house now, my girl,' he would say, and hearing those words with their barely concealed meaning, I felt myself cringe.

During half-term he took time off work. 'I want to spend a little time with my special girl,' he said to my grandmother, who smiled and said she thought his attempt to get closer to me was a very good idea. When I returned home from school for the start of the short holiday he was already at the house, waiting for me.

The curtains were drawn back in all the rooms for, until dusk fell, it would have looked strange to the neighbours if they were left closed. Pete had described to me how the neighbours had known of our mother's death: Nana had drawn the curtains on the day she had died.

'Sally, come into the hall with me.' Without waiting for an answer, he drew me by the arm into the small dark square between the front door and the two downstairs rooms. It was the one part of the house that no curious eyes could see into and, standing there, I sensed an excitement in him I hadn't seen before.

He turned me around and bent my body. With the second stair supporting my weight I wriggled in protest at having my bottom so unceremoniously sticking up into the air. His hand grabbed the back of my neck and pressed my face towards the dusty stair carpet.

'Keep still,' he commanded, and his free hand shot under my school skirt. With one tug he pulled my knickers down to my ankles. I screeched with shock as he spat. Then I felt his finger slide inside me and I cried out with pain and indignation.

'You'll soon be ready,' he crooned. 'Yep, nearly ready for me to make you a proper woman.' I felt the familiar hard thing against my buttocks as he manoeuvred it between my legs. 'You like that, don't you, my dirty little girl?' His thrusts got faster and harder with every word he gasped out. My knees seemed to have crumpled and while he supported my tummy to keep my bottom in the air my head had collapsed forward and my cheek was rubbing against the carpet. Dust and fluff seemed to fill my nose and with each thrust my breath became more restricted and my chest began to tighten.

The pressure made it seem as if the back of my throat was closing up, and as he felt me struggle for air, he moved against me harder. When he finally grunted and cried out, he stood up and I felt moisture between the cheeks of my bottom and running down my legs. My limp body slipped down the first few stairs and he left me lying on the floor gasping, only to return a few moments later with my asthma inhaler. 'Just two puffs, Sally, like the nurse showed you,' he told me, holding it towards me. I took it and squirted it inside my mouth and to the back of my throat.

Hungrily I sucked in the air it had released into my constricted lungs.

'Now say, "Thank you, Daddy. Thank you for getting my medicine."'

I looked up at him and, frightened by the expression on his face, I said what he was determined to make me say. 'Thank you, Daddy,' I replied. Then, slowly and painfully, I got to my feet on legs that wobbled and almost seemed not to be mine. Shakily I picked up my crumpled knickers and took myself to the bathroom to wash. I tore off sheets of toilet paper and rubbed everywhere he had touched, until my skin felt sore. Then I went downstairs, picked up Dolly and took her into the garden.

That night he waited until I was asleep before coming into my bedroom. 'No, please, Daddy,' I begged him, when he woke me. 'I don't want to.' He took no notice and just turned on my bedside lamp. For the first time I saw the naked body of my father.

His chest was covered with thick matted hair and the hard thing, which was so much bigger than Billy's, stood out from his body and was purple and swollen.

'Open your mouth for me, Sally,' he commanded.

Realizing what he wanted to do, I clenched my teeth, shook my head furiously and tried to beg him again not to do it. But whatever pleas I managed to get out of my mouth, he took no notice. Instead, without saying another word, he gripped my face and forced my clamped lips apart. Then he pushed the hard thing against them.

I tried to keep my teeth together as he rubbed it against my mouth. He took my fingers and placed them around it.

'Sally, if you don't want me to shove this inside you like I did my finger,' he said, touching me under my nightdress to show me exactly where he meant, 'then do what I tell you and open your bloody mouth.' Shaking with fear at his threat, I unclenched my teeth.

Angry tears spurted from my eyes and I choked when he pushed it into my open mouth. His hands reached towards my head and tangled in my hair as he moved my head backwards and forwards. The smell of him filled my nose and I felt as if I was choking. Then, just before his body buckled and shuddered, he pulled it out. Slimy smelly fluid covered my mouth and face and dribbled down the front of my nightdress. Regardless of his scrutiny, I spat and spat to get rid of the horrid taste that filled my mouth. I wanted to make sure that the slime did not go down my throat.

After he had gone I lay shaking, feeling numb and sick. Dolly crept on to the bed and I clung to her as I sobbed. Once I heard his snores I went to the bathroom to clean my teeth and rinse my mouth furiously. The taste and smell still remained, and in desperation I chewed the edge of the soap until I retched. But nothing I did that night or on subsequent ones made me feel clean.

Chapter Thirty-seven

Sue started to become a regular visitor to our house, just brief visits that never lasted more than an hour or so, but always long enough for me to see how much she wanted to be in control. Each time she and my father sat down for tea, my grandmother fussed over them and I found myself comparing Sue unfavourably to my mother.

While my mother had been vulnerable, Sue was brittle and assured. My mother's laugh had been melodic, but Sue's was high and tinkling. My mother always smiled at me with eyes softened by love, but Sue's remained hard and indifferent. She might have said that she knew we would be friends, but I saw no effort on her part to put those words into action. When she thought I wasn't looking I saw her push Dolly roughly away, and wrinkle her nose when she saw the little dog jump up against my legs for attention. Every time I sat down for tea she checked that my hands had been washed. I envied Billy his apparent indifference to her remarks, but he had learnt to save his energy for getting what he really wanted: more juice or sweets, which earned whoever gave them to him a beatific smile.

My anger with her for having taken my mother's place left me glowering, and I wished that she would go away and leave us alone. I resented her comments and disliked how often I heard her saying that animals shouldn't be allowed into the kitchen when food was being prepared or eaten. In fact, she suggested they should be outside, where I knew Dolly would be for the duration of Sue's visit, if she had her way.

'Just thinking of you, Sally,' she said, on more than one occasion. 'Your father told me you're delicate and we don't want you catching anything from the dirt she brings in, do we?'

Apart from her comments about Dolly, her conversation, which was interspersed with her shallow laugh, was entirely about her wedding plans. The first time the wedding was mentioned I had frozen and stared, bewildered, at Nana and then at my father. Receiving no denial or reassurance, I ran out into the garden with Dolly hot on my heels. I sat on the step hugging her and crying into her fur. Her cold nose pressed against my cheek and her little pink tongue licked away the tears. I didn't want a new mother, certainly not Sue, I wanted my old daddy all to myself – but if he married then maybe, just maybe, the visits to my bedroom would stop.

My grandmother came outdoors and gently closed the door behind her. She tried to comfort me, and when I asked if it was true, she said, 'Your daddy did tell you and Pete you were to have a new mother, didn't he, Sally?' I nodded slowly. He had been telling us he was planning to get married. 'You must be excited for your daddy, Sally. You and Billy need a mother and I'm getting too old to cope with Billy as much as I have to do. Come back inside, Sally, and don't be a baby.'

I returned silently to the table and sat miserably as Sue held court about the wedding plans, oblivious to my suffering.

It was to be in the town where her parents lived, the same town, she said, where my father would soon be working. This statement was dropped carelessly into the conversation and I looked at my grandmother to see if this was news to her. She made no comment and didn't even look surprised, so I took no notice of it. I was still trying to process the idea that the wedding between them was now a reality.

'Sally, you're going to be one of my bridesmaids,' she told me blithely, then went on to describe the dress I would be wearing. A long turquoise one with frills around the hem. 'And Billy will just look adorable in the little turquoise suit I'm going to have made especially for him.' Casting a smile in his direction, she added, 'And I'm getting him a bow-tie as well. He'll be the only little boy there. He'll look a proper little man.' Another high-pitched tinkling laugh rang out.

Finally the wedding date was set for late September. I was to be the only bridesmaid from our side of the family and the other four, whom I had never met before, were the daughters of Sue's friends. Three weeks before the wedding I was taken to the dressmaker for my first fitting. I had to stand still as seams and hem were pinned, and although I found it boring I had mixed emotions: every little girl wants to be a bridesmaid, but not necessarily to their father's new wife.

'One more dress check the day before the wedding. You and Billy can get ready at your granny's house,' she told me, 'and come to my house just before we leave for the church. You'll meet the other bridesmaids then.'

I had hoped I would be taken there earlier. My school-mates had described their own bridesmaid experiences and the fun of all the bridesmaids dressing together, photographs being posed for and helping the bride before setting off. I dreaded going into the church surrounded by strangers, but it was clear that that was not Sue's plan. I was disappointed but I knew better than to say anything.

A week before the wedding, Sue told me that we were going to have a 'girls' day out' before she left us to have an early night. 'The future bride needs her beauty sleep before her big day.

'Last-minute shopping, Sally,' she said, with one of those lipstick and teeth-filled smiles that never seemed to reach her eyes. 'Then a trip to the hairdresser.' She picked up some of my long tresses and examined them critically. 'Don't think you've ever been, have you?'

I shook my head and told her indignantly that my mother hadn't wanted it cut.

'Well, that was when you were younger,' she replied, with a note of barely concealed exasperation in her voice at what she saw as my lack of gratitude. 'You want it to look nice for my wedding, don't you? I'm going to treat you to a pretty new hairstyle so you look as nice as all the other little girls who are bridesmaids,' she finished brightly.

Surprised at this act of togetherness and generosity, I got up early on the morning she was coming. My father was still asleep, and although for the week before the wedding, maybe not wanting dark shadows under my eyes on the great day, he had left me alone, I was wary of waking him. I tiptoed to the bathroom to wash and clean my teeth, then put on my best dress. I sat in the lounge to make sure I was ready for her when she arrived.

She gave me a quick inspection, then said I still had

tangles in the back of my hair. Grudgingly, she picked up my brush and ran it through the offending section. 'That's the last time I'll have to do that,' she said. I didn't know what she meant.

The moment she was satisfied I looked tidy, she bundled me into her purple Mini and drove us into the nearby big town. She was a much faster driver than my father and my hands clutched at the seat as we flew round the corners on the narrow country roads.

When we arrived, she parked in front of one of the town's large department stores. 'Come along, Sally, we have things to do!' We went for her last-minute shopping, which mainly consisted of her trying out different shades of makeup. Perfume, blusher, eye shadows and lipsticks, along with a stick of pale foundation and an assortment of bottles and jars of the latest in skin care, were parcelled up and paid for before we made our way to the hairdresser. I was amazed to see her purse was brimming with money and she laughed as she handed over a fistful of cash. 'My daddy's treat to his favourite only daughter!'

In the bright lights of the chrome-and-glass-filled hairdresser's I was seated in a huge white leather chair and a bright pink towel was draped around my shoulders. The music was turned up really loud and 'Whiter Shade Of Pale' blared out of the speakers. Sue sat alongside me and sang along to the music as the manicurist prepared to file her long nails. 'So what are we doing for you today, little lady?' asked the stylist.

Before I could open my mouth to say I didn't want it changed much, Sue whisked a page from a magazine out of her handbag and proceeded to show the hairdresser a picture of something I couldn't see. 'That's how I want my future stepdaughter's hair cut,' she instructed, and the hairdresser lifted and examined my waist-length white-blonde hair.

It wasn't until I saw the large silver scissors in her hand that I realized what was going to happen.

Snip, snip, they went, and lock after lock of my treasured hair fell to the floor. I shrieked with horror as I saw how much was being cut off. The one thing my mother had loved above all else was my hair. I pictured myself sitting on her knee and her saying, 'One hundred strokes, Sally,' then slowly brushing it as her hand rested on my shoulder.

'Oh, for goodness' sake, don't be such a baby, Sally!' Sue scolded, but nothing was going to stop the tears running down my face.

The hairdresser stopped cutting when it was just below my ears.

'That looks nice now, doesn't it? Much easier for you to look after,' Sue said, as the hairdresser held up a mirror so I could see the back of my head reflected. I didn't think it looked nicer and decided that she'd meant it would be easier for her. At that moment I realized she was going to try to replace my mother in every way.

The second stop was the dressmaker, and I had my last fitting for my dress. 'You look so lovely, dear,' the seamstress said kindly, but when I looked in the mirror all I could see was a pale face still childishly round, topped by ugly short hair.

Chapter Thirty-eight

The Indian summer that we had been enjoying throughout September ended on the day of the wedding. Instead of waking up to sunlight filtering through my curtains, there was a dull grey light. Crawling out of bed I looked out of the window at thick, heavy clouds that promised rain. 'Come on, Sally. Time to get you off to your grandmother's house for her to get you ready,' my father said, flashing me one of his rare 'old-daddy' smiles.

After a breakfast of toast and Marmite with a glass of milk, he dropped me at Nana's house where Billy and I were to be dressed in our new outfits. As soon as I walked through the front door I saw the look of shock on my aunt and grandmother's faces. 'What's happened to your beautiful hair?' asked my aunt, as soon as my father had closed the door behind him.

'Sue took me to the hairdresser's yesterday,' I said glumly. 'She said it would look nice for the wedding and be easier for me to manage afterwards.'

'Ump, easier for her, more like,' I heard my aunt say, in a tone I had heard many months before: she had used it when she had criticized my mother. I knew instantly that she was the one person in the family that Sue had not managed to win over.

'Well, it's too short to plait, but I know what we'll do.' She disappeared into her bedroom and came back with a strip of turquoise velvet ribbon and a length of elastic. A needle appeared and she stitched busily until, within a few minutes, she was holding a hairband. 'This will go with your pretty dress,' she said, bestowing a smile on me. 'We'll soon have you looking nice.'

A bath was run for me, with bubbles for a treat, and once I was dry, I dressed myself in the clothes that were laid out. My aunt combed my hair and put on the velvet band to keep it in place, then declared I was ready.

My grandmother brought Billy downstairs. Wearing a miniature version of a grown-up's suit and the bow-tie, he did look very cute. Then, warning us not to move a muscle, she and my aunt went to change into their outfits of smart dresses and matching jackets. My nana's was in navy blue Crimplene, my aunt's pale yellow, and their heads were adorned with the matching floppy hats they had found on an outing to Littlewoods. When the rest of my father's family arrived, the small house seemed to be bursting with relatives of all ages. The younger girls, taking little notice that the weather had changed, wore pretty dresses. I looked enviously at my cousins in the latest Laura Ashley prints – I hated my bridesmaid attire. The boys, like their fathers, wore suits while my two other aunts were dressed in a similar fashion to my grandmother and her unmarried daughter.

My grandfather, who refused to wear anything but the dark grey suit he had worn to church for as long as I could remember, appeared from the kitchen. He had been getting some peace and quiet, he said, to read the newspaper. He was to drive my father's car and drop Billy and me at Sue's house before going to the church with Nana and my aunt. My father was to go directly to the church with my uncle, who was his best man. The rest of the family were following them in a motley assortment of cars.

My father was the last to arrive back at the house and I gasped at how smart he and his brother were looking. Both wore pale grey suits with wide lapels and fashionably flared trousers. Their shirts were purple, their wide kipper ties pale pink, and on their feet they wore gleaming black shoes. I noticed that instead of buttons my father's shirt cuffs were held together with gold links. 'A present from Sue,' he told my grandmother, when he noticed her admiring them. He looked especially striking that day, with his dark brown hair falling almost to his shoulders and his eyes sparkling in anticipation of his second marriage.

My grandmother clearly thought so too. 'Oh, Dave, you do look handsome,' she said. 'Doesn't he, Dad?'

'He looks well enough,' was the only answer she received from my grandfather.

My aunt tucked her arm into my father's and looked up at him adoringly. 'I hope Sue knows how lucky she is,' she said.

'Of course she does,' he replied laughingly, then complimented her and my grandmother effusively on their appearance.

'Now, doesn't your daughter look nice?' Nana said and, without meeting my eyes, his gaze slid quickly over my dress and short hair.

'Yes, of course, very nice,' he said, and turned to organize the synchronized setting-off to the church. Crestfallen, I followed them out to the cars. With my father and the best man leading, we drove out of the street in our raggedy convoy. Only the dress of the passengers and the white ribbons on the bonnets indicated that a celebration was about to occur.

Once we arrived at the house where Sue and her parents lived, Billy and I were quickly handed over to her mother, who took us into a room where I found all the other bridesmaids, in identical dresses to mine. Before I had time to speak to any of them she gave me a quick inspection, tweaked my dress straight, smoothed my hair, and then we were being ushered to the large black cars that had been hired for the occasion. Sue came out of the house, the train of her white dress held in one hand, and climbed into the first, which was decked out in wide white ribbons. The other girls chatted on the way to the church but it was clear they were not interested in Billy or me.

At the church I watched as Sue's father, a tall thin man with a wide false-teeth-white smile and sparse grey hair combed neatly back from a high forehead, climbed out of the car. He leant in and held out his arm to help his daughter alight. Yards of white lace made up the train we had to lift and a short veil hid Sue's face, but I could see that her hair was arranged in a French pleat with loose tendrils brushing against her cheeks and that drop diamanté earrings glittered in her lobes.

I heard the music change and the Bridal March start. I saw backs straighten and Sue turned to us to show she was ready to make her entrance. I copied what the other bridesmaids did and positioned myself at the side of the train. On a signal from the matron of honour, we lifted the heavy lace fabric and slowly walked behind the bride and her father into the flower-decked church. Billy had been told to hold a basket of rose petals and throw them as he walked with us. He looked very serious as he flung his handfuls on to the floor.

When we got halfway down the aisle he stopped, realizing the basket was empty. 'Come on, Billy, keep walking,' the matron of honour instructed, in a loud whisper.

Every pew seemed to be full, but I saw that the church was jammed with people I didn't recognize. Sue's family and friends took up more than two-thirds of the space.

I searched the faces that were turned towards us for my older brother and knew that Pete had been true to his word: he had not turned up to see his father remarry. I wished he had because I needed him so much. Only he would understand what it was like to see my father remarry so soon after my mother's death.

I dimly heard the words of the service and followed the lead of the other bridesmaids when necessary. I saw the best man patting his pockets, then passing the wedding ring to my father. He put it on Sue's outstretched hand. I watched her lift her veil and raise her face as his head bent and he kissed her. I knew then that, like it or not, she had just become my new mother.

After what seemed like an age they returned from signing the register and, to a fanfare of organ music, my father swiftly led the procession out of the church with his new wife. The other bridesmaids, Billy and I followed and stood on the steps, while the photographer aimed his camera at us.

As we looked towards him a strong gust of wind lifted Sue's veil and blew it across her face. When she pushed it back I noticed a smear of pink lipstick had stained it. All around us ladies' gloved hands were raised to anchor hats that the wind tried to wrench from their heads, and girls shrieked as they clutched the hems of their pretty floaty dresses. That, I thought, will be one photograph that won't be put in the album, and again I wished Pete was there to catch my eye. Later we would have giggled together at the sight of the one hat that got away. It was a cream one, shaped like a wheel and trimmed with black flowers. It took on a life of its own and sailed over our heads. Dipping and rising in the wind, it went halfway across the churchyard in a moment, and it took the agility of the best man, sprinting, to retrieve it. With a little bow, he returned it to its owner who, intent on stopping her skirt blowing above her head, had let go of it.

But Pete and I would not share these events because he wasn't there. He had stuck to his word and had categorically refused to come.

The clouds kept to their earlier promise and rain started to fall in ever-increasing strength. A huge black umbrella appeared and was held over Sue's head to protect her from the large drops as we made our way quickly to the fleet of awaiting limousines. We climbed in and were driven to the very posh country-house hotel that Sue had chosen for the reception.

As we went up the long tree-lined driveway, my grandmother told me that the hotel had once been a stately home, the largest in the county. When I looked up I saw rows of tall windows and imposing stone steps leading up to huge wooden front doors. The staircase was flanked by white pillars on either side and I wondered how big the family had been who had once lived there. Inside the

entrance hall there was a magnificent chandelier. Its sparkling drops were almost blinding with their dazzling
brilliance. The acres of carpet were soft and spongy to
walk on and the air was thick with the perfume of the tall
flower arrangements that stood on every table.

When we reached what was grandly called the Banqueting Suite there were long damask-covered tables
arranged in a horseshoe shape with more flowers, silver
cutlery, white linen napkins and crystal glasses. I remembered the rare times my mother had tried to make our own
little dinner table look pretty. Looking round me at all the
people this room was ready to hold, I was bewildered by its
size and even Nana seemed rather overwhelmed. 'There
must be over two hundred guests here,' she whispered in
amazement to my granddad.

'Bet she don't even know them all!' he scoffed.

I was placed at a table with the other bridesmaids and
Billy, while my grandparents sat with Sue, her parents, my
father, the best man, the matron of honour and a few
people I didn't know.

Discreet waiters served the start of the three-course
meal. The wine flowed but on our table there were jugs of
juice. The other bridesmaids, two pairs of sisters who had
known each other all their lives, giggled together, and I
was left with Billy for company. He already looked droopy-
eyed with tiredness, so I sat and watched everything that
was taking place around me.

I ate the food that was put in front of me without enthusiasm. When the main course was finished we sat back as
they announced that the speeches would take place now.

I heard the popping of champagne corks as bottles

were opened ready for the toasts. Sue's father's speech seemed to go on and on about how he had not lost a daughter but gained a business partner. My uncle, the best man, cracked a couple of jokes about when he and my father had been younger; jokes that, despite the adults' laughter, I didn't understand. He went on to say how delighted our family was to have Sue join it. He toasted the bridesmaids, and then it was my father's turn to praise his new bride and repeat the best man's sentiments in reverse, that he was so pleased to be part of his new family.

The rain had finally stopped and the sun came out so we were quickly taken into the grounds for the main photographs. More pictures were taken of the happy couple with the bridesmaids and Billy. Last the photographer grouped both families together and snapped away. Later when I looked at them in Sue's album I saw a picture of my grandmother smiling happily, my grandfather looking almost as bored as I felt, and the best man appeared to be a little drunk with his tie askew and his hair windswept.

We returned to the Banqueting Suite to see that the faces of those who had remained behind had grown pinker, their laughter higher, and the air had become dense with cigar and cigarette smoke. The music struck up and the band leader asked us all to stand as my father led Sue back into the room and on to the dance floor for the first dance. The other bridesmaids sneaked off to join their families and I sat immobilized by stultifying boredom, waiting for someone to notice Billy and me on our own. It was my grandmother who moved us. Sue and my father were intent on each other and their guests – they appeared to have forgotten our existence.

Later Sue and my father disappeared to change, she into a pretty cream suit while my father wore a pair of fawn slacks and a pale blue open-necked shirt.

'Come on, we have to go outside to wave them off,' said my grandmother and, taking Billy's hand, she led us from the room, following many of the other guests, out to the front steps.

Amid gales of laughter people were throwing confetti as my father, with his arm around his new wife's waist, ran for the car under the shower of multicoloured paper. I heard the rattle of the tin cans that were tied to the back and watched as they drove off together, giving their friends and family one last wave.

It was then that it dawned on me they were gone, not just down the road, but on their honeymoon, and they hadn't said goodbye to either Billy or me. My fingers curled around my grandmother's and I moved closer to her side.

'I think it's time we got you two home,' my grandfather said, and I knew that he had noticed his son and his new wife's indifference to us.

Chapter Thirty-nine

As my grandparents hadn't a spare room for me to sleep in, it had been arranged that Nana would sleep in our house and Billy would come with her. Part of me wished that my father's honeymoon would last for ever. Nana made sure that a hot breakfast was put in front of me every morning and, even though I was old enough to take myself there, she and Billy walked with me to school. She let me put Dolly on a lead and then took her from me when we reached the school gates. When school finished she and Billy were back again, accompanied by my little dog whose front feet furiously pawed the air as she stood on her hind legs in delight at seeing me.

The two weeks that my father and Sue were away went by too quickly for me, and it was on the Sunday after we had returned from church that they reappeared. My grandmother had decided to cook the lunch at her house because 'There's nothing like your own stove to do a roast,' and, besides, her dining-table had leaves that extended to seat more people than our small kitchen table. As well as her daughter and my grandfather, she had also invited my uncle, who had been best man, his wife and two children, who were just a few years older than me, to join us. I had been given the task of laying the table and was busy putting out knives and forks when they walked in.

There was a flurry of hellos, hugs for Billy and me from both of them amid excited chatter about the Lake District where they had spent their honeymoon. They said that although it had been cold it was beautiful. Then we squeezed, shoulder to shoulder, around the table, which was almost groaning under the weight of the food.

'Shame you missed church, Sue. The minister gave such a good sermon today,' my grandmother said, and received a wide-eyed look of disbelief from Sue.

'Oh, church isn't something I bother about,' she said, with the little laugh that grated on me. 'Of course I always do go at Christmas and Easter,' she added, when she saw the look of disapproval settling on my grandmother's face. 'But Sunday is the one day that David and I can spend together. Isn't it, darling?' She turned her adoring gaze on my father.

He looked embarrassed. Not only did his whole family attend church regularly but he took pleasure in knowing his Bible and, as I had learnt to my detriment, used passages from it to reinforce his wishes.

'Let's talk about this later, dear,' he said quietly to her. 'Sue works very hard all week,' he said. 'Being her father's assistant doesn't mean he grants her any favours and sometimes she has to go in on Saturday mornings. So Sunday is her only real day off.' I wondered, as I thought of her brand new purple Mini with its custom-made leather seats and the cassette player under the dashboard, her expensive clothes and jewellery and the lavish wedding, what my father meant by her not being granted any favours. I knew from remarks I had heard that those things were not paid for out of a normal secretary's salary.

Whatever was said when they did talk in private, it was one battle Sue didn't win: the next Sunday she put in an appearance at church. But I was blissfully unaware of all her other plans for our family.

It was my grandmother who collected me from the house and took me to Sunday school that day. My father and Sue were to join them at church later. It was also my grandmother who pointed out to my father that I was growing fast and needed some new clothes for school; a comment he repeated to Sue later.

'Your children have enough clothes and toys,' she said. 'You work so hard for your money and you don't want to waste it, do you, David?'

Before he could answer her, Sue, knowing his reluctance to go against anything his mother asked for, put her arm round his shoulders and bent down to rest her face against his. 'You know I'm only saying it because I love you, don't you?' She received a smile of agreement.

'Anyhow, I had lunch with Daddy today and I've got some wonderful news to tell you. So don't make any plans yet about getting Sally any new school clothes.'

I watched my father's face light up and knew that, whatever Sue had to tell him, he had already guessed.

'And, David, while we're on the subject of your children, Sally needs to help out more. She spends all her time playing with that dog.' He glanced at me to see if I was listening but said nothing in my defence.

I felt resentful of her criticism. I did as much as I could to help after school and at weekends. Billy now slept in the house in Pete's old room while my grandmother and aunt still looked after him during the day. I helped him dress and undress in the mornings and evenings, and I amused him while Sue polished her nails or flicked through a glossy magazine.

Chapter Forty

A few weeks later I found out why my school uniform had to wait. The wonderful surprise was that we were moving. Sue's father had bought them a brand new house and the building work had just been completed. It was now almost ready to move into. Evidently part of his business was near to where he lived and he needed someone to run it, and Sue had persuaded him that not only was her new husband the right person for the job but that she would be happier living nearer to her parents. It became clear that my father had known all this before the wedding and that they had just been waiting for their house, which was on a new estate, to be finished. Neither Pete nor I nor our grandparents had known of this.

When I first heard we were going to live in a new house, I thought my father meant in another part of our village. 'Where is it?' I asked, thinking it was going to be one of the new Wimpy homes that were springing up like mushrooms on the outskirts of our village. To my dismay, I was told that we were moving right away from all that was familiar to near where the wedding had been.

'You'll love it, Sally,' my father said, in the tone he had used when he had told me I would love having a new mummy. He had been wrong about that and I was convinced he would be wrong about this.

Noticing that my face had not broken into a wide smile

of joy, Sue chipped in. Her firm tone told me it would be useless to argue with her: 'Sally, it's where your daddy's going to work now, so it makes sense. Anyhow, you'll have a lovely surprise when you see it. The house is beautiful and everything's going to be brand new.' But however much Sue gushed and my father enthused, I could only stare at them in horror. We were moving from our house, the one my mother had loved, the only one that Billy and I had ever called home.

'But what about going to school?' I asked, for some reason not taking it in that there were schools in every town and that that would be the least of my problems.

I was told that I was already enrolled in a new one and that Billy's name had been put down for the infants. 'He'll be old enough to start there in a few months,' she added.

It was then that her words sank in. The thought of not having my grandmother on the doorstep terrified me.

'You'll make lots of new friends there,' she said, with confidence, ignoring the fact that it was my cousins I played with, not my classmates.

'What about Nana?' I said.

'Oh, you'll be able to visit her and she can visit you,' was the answer, and my heart sank even further, for Nana was the one person in my life who I knew loved me. I thought of the journey to the wedding and how long it had taken. My grandparents didn't own a car and I knew it would take hours for them to get to us by bus.

The thought of only having Sue and my father to care for me made me feel as though a dark hole was opening up beneath my feet. On the pretext of going to my grandmother's house I went to wait for Pete to return to his digs after he finished work.

'That was her plan all along, I bet,' he said angrily, when I told him of Sue's announcement. 'She didn't want to live near our grandparents because she wants Dad all to herself. Selfish bitch! She doesn't care about you or Billy. Anyhow, I bet she doesn't think they're good enough for her. And her sort certainly doesn't want to be seen living on a council estate.' Although my brother had refused to speak to my father since he had heard of the wedding plans and hadn't met his new stepmother, he had observed her from a distance and formed his own unflattering opinions.

I found out much later that Pete was right in all respects. Sue's father had offered to put mine in charge of the local business operation and helped them buy the house in the village. My father's only concern had been the effect on his marriage of uprooting two young children who had lost their mother from their extended family. But, most of all, he knew by now that Sue was not a natural mother and he was concerned with moving Billy and me away from the grandmother who had cared for us.

It was Sue herself who told me, in one of her nasty bitchy outbursts, but not until much later. She had seen my grandmother as interfering and the rest of my father's family as common and overbearing. She had been determined to start her married life well away from them, even if it meant she had to look after Billy and me.

But at the time, of course, I was too young to understand and was totally unaware of it when I talked to my brother.

'You'll just have to accept it, Sally,' he said, when he looked at my dismal face. Bitterly he continued, 'There's no way she wants to stay here. Dad's fallen on his feet, all right, hasn't he? As soon as Mum's buried he wants to show off Sue. Of course her dad bought that house for them. He's rolling in it – the lads at work told me. I 'spect she can get anything she wants off him. She's the only daughter and, from what I've heard, she's got him wrapped round her little finger.'

As he saw the tears welling in my eyes my brother reached out his arm and drew me to him. 'Don't worry, Sally, we'll still see each other when you come to visit Nana,' he said, giving me a little hug. 'I'll miss you and Billy, but I'm pleased I'm not going too.' He gave me another hug, then walked towards the door of the friend's house where he was staying. I watched him as he slouched along with his hands in his pockets but he didn't turn round. I realized that he, too, was lonely and that it wasn't just my grandmother I was going to miss.

'Can't I stay here with you?' I asked my grandmother plaintively, the next time I saw her. 'I don't want to move away from you – I need you, Nana, and so does Billy.'

'Sally, you know you have to go with them,' was the answer she gave.

'Well, if you don't want me, what about Aunt Janet? She does, I know she does. She's said so.'

'Sally, stop this nonsense. Your daddy wants you and so does Sue,' she exclaimed.

At that I burst into tears and told her again that I didn't want to move. 'I'll never see you,' I said. 'Why have we got to move? What's wrong with our house?' My voice broke and I started sobbing. As my body shook with despair all I could think was that with the move I would have no one left.

Nana told me firmly not to be silly and to dry my eyes. Of course I would see her often. I would come to visit and she would come to our new house as well.

I looked at her dubiously; her words with their unsteady lack of conviction seemed as much for her as for me. 'But it won't be the same,' I howled, and to that she had no answer for, of course, it wouldn't be. She knew I was moving away from everything that was familiar and all remnants of my mother.

'Sally, Sue's father has helped them buy a lovely new house. It has a large garden and Dolly's going to like having more space to run around in, isn't she?'

'I suppose,' I mumbled, as I tried to staunch the tears. That Dolly was coming was some consolation.

It was then that she gave me the photograph of my mother; the one that showed her windswept and smiling. She had put it in a pretty gilt frame especially for me. 'I thought you'd like to take this with you,' she said. I ran my fingers slowly over the glass, stroking her features, and thought longingly of her.

Chapter Forty-one

One Saturday morning I sat moping at the kitchen table. Dolly was outside in the garden as Sue had banned her from the kitchen while we ate or prepared food. As Sue was drinking her coffee and nibbling at dry toast, she dropped another bombshell.

Her large magnifying mirror was propped against the cereal box and she squinted as, tweezers in hand, she looked for any hair that might have sprung up to disturb the narrow line of an eyebrow. I stared, fascinated – my mother had never done anything like this. Eventually she glanced at me. 'Oh, Sally,' she said pleasantly. 'I've been meaning to talk to you about Dolly.' Almost as though she had heard her name, my dog started whining to be let in. Sue studiously ignored her. 'I think we'll have to look for another home for her when we go to the new house.'

'No!' I said, shocked.

'Well, Sally, I know you're very fond of her, but she might not like a move.'

I didn't believe that Sue was in the least bit bothered about Dolly's feelings. If she wasn't concerned about mine, she would scarcely consider a little dog's. 'She likes being with me, wherever I am,' I said stubbornly.

Light grey eyes steadily held mine, and a slim hand rested briefly on my wrist. I knew that this was one battle I couldn't let her win. 'I can't let her go. She was a special present from Daddy,' I said. 'He gave her to me and he loves her too!'

'He gave her to you when you were still upset about your mother,' she replied quickly, 'but now that we're moving to a new house and a new life, things will be different for you. And you have me as your mummy now.'

The instinct for self-preservation told me to be quiet and bide my time. It was my father I would have to get round, and I decided to wait until we were all together at the table to tackle him. Making Sue really angry wasn't going to help me or Dolly.

Thinking that my silence meant she had won, Sue put down her tweezers and focused on painting her nails pale pink with slow, careful strokes.

'Daddy,' I said, when he came and sat down, 'I can't let Dolly be given away and go to another home when we move. I just can't.'

I saw by the almost guilty expression that came over his face that he and Sue had already discussed the little dog's fate.

'Well, Sue thought –'

I gave him no chance to repeat her words. I just turned my face so I was looking directly at him and stared him in the eyes. 'But, Daddy, you gave her to me. You remember the day when you said she was mine, don't you?' I held his gaze.

He did, I saw that – and I also knew that he recalled only too clearly the day he had brought her home and what had followed in my bedroom later. Since his marriage his hands had not touched me but his eyes had. Too often I had caught him looking at my legs under their short skirts not to be aware of what he was thinking about. I watched his face closely because I knew he remembered the real reason that Dolly had become part of our family.

I heard Sue say, 'David,' as she tried to regain his attention. I heard her say something about new cream carpets and germs, but for once he took no notice of her as we stared each other out.

'Oh, all right! She can stay, but you make sure you look after her. Sue has quite enough to do,' he said finally. I felt a surge of something like power. At last I had manipulated a situation in my favour.

'Oh, Davie darling, I thought we'd agreed,' Sue said, with a hint of barely concealed annoyance.

'Well, Sally does love her. I really didn't think she'd mind so much.'

That, I knew, was a lie. He just hadn't thought I would stand up to him. 'As long as Sally looks after her and she stays outside or in the kitchen, of course,' he added.

I saw a flash of rage cross Sue's face and knew that she would be unforgiving at having lost the argument over Dolly. But it was worth it if I could keep my beloved little dog.

Chapter Forty-two

We moved at the weekend. The night before we left I had packed up my room and Billy's. I had put our clothes in suitcases, and his toys and my books fitted into two cardboard boxes. Then we had all gone to my grandmother's house for supper. Just as Sue had once monopolized the conversation with her wedding plans, now she enthused non-stop about the new house.

As usual my grandfather said very little, just commented that it all sounded very nice, but my normally talkative grandmother was unusually quiet. When we left and returned home I felt sad and dispirited. I wondered if I would ever again have a meal with all of the family members I loved so much.

The next morning, after a rushed breakfast, suitcases were piled into Sue's and my father's cars. My grandmother arrived to say goodbye, but after a cup of tea Sue looked at her watch and said it was time to leave.

'What about everything else?' I asked.

'Oh, someone's coming to take it all away,' Sue said airily.

I looked at the settee where I had sat with my mother, at the cushions I had watched her making, and remembered the lovely blue quilt on my bed, which she had tucked around me at night. Surely Sue couldn't mean that nothing else was coming with us. 'But what about . . .' I was thinking of all the china and ornaments my mother had loved and the bits of silver I had polished with her.

Sue waved a hand at me in a gesture that told me to be quiet. 'Sally, we're going to have lovely new stuff. We don't need all this tat,' she said impatiently.

Then we were outside and I watched as the meagre sum of the possessions Sue had allowed us to take was packed into the two cars. With Sue following behind I sat next to my father on the long drive to where the new house was. It was at the end of a cul-de-sac where another five identical houses stood. With its red bricks and wooden window-frames, it looked like a smaller version of Sue's parents' house. There was a lawn at the front and a double garage at the side, and when I walked round it I saw that outside the french windows there was a tiled patio and more lawn and garden.

Sue was bursting with pride as my father opened the front door. 'First rule of the house, children. We all take our shoes off as we come in. Hurry up now, I want to give you the tour,' she said, and I saw my father was already untying his laces. By the front door on a neat mat lay an assortment of cotton slippers. Pointing at the second smallest pair, Sue said, 'Those are yours, Sally. Now, help Billy with his too, please.'

It was the most pristine house I had ever seen. Cream carpets covered the stairs and hall while the floor of the L-shaped room that Sue insisted I called 'the lounge' was covered with a thick white shag pile rug. I thought that if Dolly did manage to get in there, which I already knew was strictly forbidden, we would never see her. 'Second rule of the house – remember, Sally, what we told you?

No dogs. Also, no toys, no food or drinks are allowed in here,' Sue chanted. It seemed there were going to be strict rules for each and every room.

The new furniture was already in place. Two white leather settees, a chrome-and-glass coffee-table, shelves with crystal figurines and grey and white pottery figures, which Sue told me proudly were something called 'Lladro'. A bar shaped like a globe stood in a corner and my father opened it to show me the assortment of bottles inside. Against the wall near to an imitation stone fireplace, there was another shelving unit where the new eight-track stereo system stood. A completely round white television on a white stand was on the carpet. It was unlike anything I had ever seen before and I wondered if Billy and I would ever be allowed to watch it.

In the dining area there was an oblong table made of a pale shiny wood with six chairs that had cream-upholstered seats. The matching sideboard was covered with framed photographs of Sue and her parents. Those of her and my father's wedding were also there, although there were no group ones showing any of our family. Pastel prints and gilt mirrors hung on the walls and at the windows there were floor-length beige velvet curtains tied back with gold tasselled cords.

With Billy trailing in our wake, Sue showed us around the rest of the house with pride. The kitchen was gleaming white with shiny stainless-steel pans on the stove, the bathroom was tiled in pale green, and Billy's room had a single bed with a brightly coloured quilt. 'You can keep all your toys in here. Nothing is to be left out,' she told him, as she opened a cupboard and left him staring in bewilderment at his new surroundings. I knew that playing anywhere downstairs would not be allowed. Then a few feet from his room she stopped and swung open the door of the room she announced was mine.

It was decorated in pink and white. My bed was covered with a pale pink frilly eiderdown and beside it stood a small table and a lamp with a pink-fringed shade. On one wall there were built-in wardrobes, some bookshelves and a small desk. 'For you to do your homework on,' she told me. 'No more having to sit at the kitchen table to do it.' She sat on the bed then, and motioned for me to sit beside her. 'Sally,' she said, 'I want you to call me Mummy from now on. You can't keep calling me Auntie Sue, can you?' Her arm went round me and I could smell her perfume, a cloying scent that I didn't like. I shifted down the bed a little – her closeness made me feel uncomfortable. 'You like your room, don't you? I chose the wallpaper myself.'

I looked at the pink-and-white-striped walls and whispered, 'Yes.' I knew she wanted more, that a flood of girlish words expressing my delight was expected, but this room with its fitted cupboards and pale carpeting was nothing like any place I had slept in before and I found it intimidating.

Her eyes slid around the room. 'I don't know any little girl who wouldn't love a bedroom of their own looking like this.'

Finally I managed the words I knew she wanted to hear. 'Thank you. It's lovely.'

'Thank you who, Sally?' she chided.

'Mummy,' I managed to force out.

'Sally, I know we're all going to be so happy here,' she

said then and, with a smile, she left me to sort out my things.

I put my books on the shelves with my Tiny Tears doll. My dolls' house, which my father had carried upstairs, went under it. Then I hung my clothes in the small white fitted wardrobe. The last thing I took out of my case was the treasured photograph of my mother. I held it for a few moments: my mother's face had become blurred in my mind and seeing her image made it clearer. I placed it on my bedside table facing my bed so that it would be the first thing I saw when I woke.

Lost in my thoughts I didn't hear Sue's footsteps so I jumped when I suddenly realized she was back in my room.

'Sally, what's this you're looking at?' she asked, and pulled the frame out of my hands.

'My mummy,' I said, and started to tell her how my grandmother had given it to me. I stopped when I saw that Sue's mouth was pursed and her eyes flashed with anger.

'Sally, I thought we'd just had a little conversation where you agreed that I'm your mummy now and I don't want you talking about any other one. Now, have you finally got that into your head? Because I don't want to have to tell you again. Do you understand me?'

'But what else can I call her?' I asked, more puzzled than alarmed at her displeasure.

'I thought your daddy had also told you not to talk about her. Hasn't he?'

'Yes. But Nana said that was because it made him sad. He didn't say I can't talk about her to anyone else.'

I knew the words I had said were the wrong ones, but I had no way of retracting them and my voice just dried up. I felt a wave of apprehension as I saw Sue's rage reflected in her face.

'Well, I don't want to hear her name again. You're not to talk about her. In fact, I want you to forget that you ever had another mummy.'

I just stared at her in shock. How could she say that to me?

'I don't want to,' I said defiantly. 'I don't want to forget my mummy. She loved me.'

'Sally, if it wasn't for me, you and Billy would have ended up in a home. You know that, don't you?'

I started to argue that my nana would have looked after us, only for her to brush that statement aside. 'Your nana's getting too old to look after small children, Sally. She told you that herself, didn't she? And it's up to me whether you stay here with us – do you understand me?'

'Yes,' I said, although I didn't really.

'Good! So, no more answering me back. Ever. Do you hear me?'

I heard her, and the words she spoke brought back the memory of how frightened I had been at the thought of being taken away from everything I loved. But Sue, in just a few short weeks, had managed to do that anyhow. Wanting to get away from her, I made movements to leave the room, which suddenly felt claustrophobic.

'Sally, before you go I want you to promise this is the last time I'll need to speak to you about this.'

I looked mutinously back at her and said nothing.

The veneer of Sue as the loving stepmother who

wanted to do her best for us disappeared, and I felt the force of her will dominate that room. I also felt it in the tight grip on my shoulder and saw it in her glare. I shrank back from her.

'Say it. Say you'll never talk about her again. I want to hear it before you leave this room!' she shrieked.

My tongue seemed to swell in my mouth, blocking the words she was trying to make me say, and all I could do was stare silently at her with my lips moving silently.

'Sally, I'm warning you! Say it!' she spat.

Against my will I managed to force the words out: 'I won't talk about her in front of you again.'

'And who am I?'

'Mummy,' I replied dutifully.

'Now if I'm your mummy, the only one you have, who is that a picture of?'

I didn't understand what she wanted me to say.

'Sally, it distresses me that you have that photograph in a room I've had decorated for you. It seems to me you're a very ungrateful little girl.'

'No, I'm not, really I'm not,' I protested, and tears threatened to spill over.

'The only thing I expect from you, Sally,' Sue continued, taking no heed of my distress, 'is that you show your gratitude and treat me with the respect I deserve. Do you understand? Then we'll get on well again. Now, you don't want to spoil our first day in our new home, do you?'

I shook my head, still not knowing what she wanted from me. I was soon to find out.

She gave me back the photograph and I went to put it in my case out of her sight.

'Oh, no, Sally! That's not what I want at all,' she said sharply. 'Here, give it back to me.'

She lifted my face with one of her slim white hands and, her sharp nails digging into my cheek, forced me to meet her gaze. 'You can show me just how grateful you really are by doing the one thing that will please me, can't you? You want to do that, don't you?'

'Yes,' I answered softly.

'Well, what I want you to do is take that photograph out of its frame and tear it up now,' she said.

'No – please, it's my only one.'

'Sally, if you care what I think you'll do what I ask of you.' She turned the frame over, undid the tiny clasps holding the photograph in place and removed it. 'I'm not leaving this room till you do this.' Feeling an all-consuming hatred for her, I did as she asked. I took one last look at my mother's features and tried with all my might to imprint her likeness for ever in my memory. As my fingers ripped the picture I watched in horror as her face became a pile of tiny jagged pieces. I wanted to cry but somehow I stopped the tears. That was the start of the invisible, impenetrable wall I built, brick by brick, between myself, Sue and everything else that hurt me.

Sue, I swore silently, was never going to see me cry again and, over the painful years that followed, she never did.

Chapter Forty-three

Apart from the first miserable days of living in the new house, everything that happened, coming up to Christmas and the few days after it, has been driven from my memory. Glimpses of those months when I was around eight sometimes float into my mind, and I can see the lounge with a tall white artificial Christmas tree in the corner. No pine needles could be allowed to fall on the new carpets, and my mother's lovely collection of old glass decorations had been abandoned when we left the old house. Sue kept arriving home with boxes and bags of sparkling new decorations, all in her colour scheme of white, silver and pink. Of course there would have been presents, but I can no longer remember what they were.

There were drinks parties that she called 'cocktails' or 'at home' for the new neighbours and her many friends. Banished to our bedrooms, Billy and I could hear laughter and the Christmas music playing in the lounge. I know we went to Sue's parents for our Christmas dinner, but all recollection of the meal has vanished from my mind.

The one thing I can recall in perfect detail is the terrible row Sue and my father had.

When my grandfather died, everything in my life began to change again. It had snowed heavily on that memorable Friday night. Great flurries of thick white flakes had fallen, carpeting the lawns and transforming the bare branches of the trees into objects of great beauty.

Christmas had come and gone and the new year had already been heralded in when we heard the terrible news. It was while we were eating breakfast that the telephone rang and my father went into the hall to answer it. I knew something was wrong even before he told us what had happened. His shoulders were slumped and the colour had drained from his face when he came back into the kitchen.

'My father's dead,' he said to Sue, forgetting that it was also the death of Billy's and my grandfather he had announced so bluntly. 'A heart attack,' he said. 'My mum thought it was indigestion and went to get him something to take and when she came back he was already dead. It happened in just those few minutes.'

When Sue asked when, he said it had been the evening before, but my grandmother had waited until the morning to ring him. 'She thought we might have been out, New Year and all,' he said, 'and she didn't want to have to tell the children or the babysitter.'

For the first time in my life I saw my father's eyes water with emotion, and with his grief came remorse and guilt. 'We should have gone for Christmas, Sue. They asked us. Mum and Dad wanted to see the children so much and they wanted to give us our presents, not send them by post like they did.'

Her reply was characteristically unsympathetic. Something about he couldn't have known it was to be his father's last Christmas and he mustn't blame himself for not going to see them.

He didn't blame himself, he shouted. He blamed her. And that was when their row started.

She was controlling, he was ungrateful, and as the shouting escalated, Billy and I slid off our seats and disappeared up to our respective rooms.

It was later that my father told me the funeral was to be in three days and, unlike my mother's, I was to go. I didn't let on that I had heard this mentioned in the row.

'Sue's not coming,' was all he said, but I had heard enough to know he didn't want her with him any more than she wanted to go. I had heard her tell him in a shrill voice, grown nearly hysterical with anger, that she didn't want to go with him and that she knew his family didn't like her. They blamed her for taking him and the children away and for not going to church.

In response to 'What on earth will I tell them if I turn up without you?' she told him to say she was looking after Billy and that he was too young to go to a funeral. He retorted that she could hardly expect them to be fond of her when she did nothing but talk about herself and her father's money, and put obstacles in his way when he wanted us to visit his parents.

More insults were hurled, and then I overheard her saying that she didn't see why he had to take me. But on that decision my father was adamant. 'She's coming with me. Her grandmother will expect to see her there. So you sort out something suitable for her to wear, do you hear me?'

So, it was just my father and I who set off a few days later for my grandmother's house. We were both silent on the long journey. He was lost in his thoughts but I, alone with him for the first time since his marriage, felt uneasy. I knew I should say something if only to tell him I was sorry my grandfather was dead, but his forbidding expression halted any thought of trying to engage him in conversation.

When we arrived, the house was already full of my aunts and uncles. My grandmother, a small shrunken figure dressed head to toe in black, suddenly looked old and frail. Her eyes, magnified behind her glasses, had once lit her face, but were now sad and unfocused. I wanted to run to her and throw my arms around her, but her grief formed a hidden barrier and stopped me. Instead, I hung back behind my aunt, who was trying hard not to cry – being brave for her mother's sake.

When the hearse and the large black cars that were to take us to the church arrived, my vulnerable grandmother stood and took my father's arm, clung to it for support as if the grief had sucked away all her strength. With her arm through his and his large gloved hand covering hers, they walked out of the house together. We all followed to where the funeral cars were waiting.

It was only when she led the way into the cold unheated church that I saw her brush aside his arm. She took a deep breath, pulled herself upright, then moved forward with her head erect and a small smile of greeting for the people who were turning to acknowledge her.

The only sound I could hear as we went to our seats at the front was the shuffling of feet and the rustling of the order of service sheets that were being handed out at the door. I looked around and saw family, friends, neighbours and many old men wearing medals, who had served in the war with my grandfather. Some came in pairs, others walked in alone, and one by one they went first to pay their respects to my grandmother. Grey heads bent to hers, soft words of sympathy were spoken and all the time she stood by the pew, thanking them for coming despite the bitterly cold weather and the treacherous icy roads.

My eyes were transfixed by the flower-covered coffin near the pulpit, and I pictured my grandfather lying asleep inside it. Every pew was full by the time our vicar indicated that the service was about to begin, and after his opening words, the choir led the congregation as the organ played and we all stood up. The church rang with the clear notes of 'The Lord Is My Shepherd'. I saw my grandmother's head rise and watched the tears that trickled down her cheeks. Then her lips started to move as she joined in, the words of my grandfather's favourite psalm comforting her.

'I am the Resurrection and the Life, saith the Lord . . .' The words floated over my head, as did the short sermon.

My aunt held a wet hanky to her face for nearly the whole of the service, but once the first hymn had been sung, my grandmother was stoically dry-eyed. My father was called upon by the minister to read a short passage from the Bible and speak about his father, as was my grandfather's closest friend of many years.

It was my father and his brothers who rolled the casket on casters down the aisle, then carried it on their shoulders back to the hearse.

We drove in convoy to the cemetery on the outskirts of town; the one where my mother was buried. I stood near my grandmother and bowed my head as the minister intoned the committal prayer: 'It has pleased Almighty

God to take from this world the soul of David East here departed,' and as he uttered the final words, 'We now commit his body to the ground,' the coffin was lowered into the deep rectangular space that had been dug for it.

'Earth to earth, ashes to ashes, dust to dust,' rang in my ears, as my grandmother and her sons threw small handfuls of earth on to the coffin. Then it was over and my grandmother took my father's arm again and walked painfully away from the new grave, in which her husband of many years now lay.

The women in the village had arranged to use the church hall to provide refreshments. Many of my grandfather's friends from his war days had travelled for miles to attend the funeral and my grandparents' house was just not big enough for all of them to gather there. We went to the hall from the cemetery to find that tea, cakes and sandwiches had been laid out. Everyone stood around in groups, remembering my grandfather and reminiscing about his life and how they had all met. I went to Nana's side and she took my hand.

Even though I had never been as close to the taciturn old man as I was to my grandmother, I felt tears come to my eyes: this was another death, which meant I would never see the person again.

She pulled me closer to her. 'He didn't suffer, Sally,' she said. 'It was very quick.'

I thought then that he might be in the magic place with my mother. 'But he can see us, can't he?' I asked, and she smiled; a smile that momentarily chased the sadness from her eyes.

'Yes, Sally,' she said, 'he can,' and I knew she remembered the story my mother had told me.

Pete came over to us – he had grown into a man in just the few months since we had last met. Once he and Nana had said a few words, he asked me how I liked the new house, but all I could think of was how much I missed my father's family. 'It's nice, Pete – well, it's all right, I suppose,' was all I could bring myself to say.

Something made me keep quiet about Sue and my father's row. In her face that morning I had recognized a look I had seen on my stepmother's face, one in which the confidence had slipped. It was that of a woman in love with her husband but no longer certain of him. I felt a surprising wave of pity for her. It was destined to be short-lived.

Chapter Forty-four

My father and I stayed until every guest had left, then returned with my grandmother to her house. I heard him promise he would be back in a week to see her.

It was early evening when we left and, tired by the emotion of the day, and made sleepy by the sudden warmth from the car's heater, which was on full blast, I fell into a doze on the seat beside him. I felt the car start to bump along and heard the note of the engine change. I opened my eyes to see that we had driven off the main road and turned down a rutted narrow lane. It led us through an area thick with trees and bushes. Tractors had cleared the snow from the road but I could see, by the light of the headlamps, that the verges were still thick with snow that was undisturbed, except for the tiny prints of birds' and other small creatures' feet. My father drove deeper into the wooded area, which the thick foliage had sheltered from the worst of the snowfall.

Briars and brambles choked the narrow path he took, and on either side of us the slender trunks of tall spruce trees had grown so close that it became darker and darker as the night closed in. We reached a small clearing and my father turned off the engine and the headlights, leaving us sitting in an eerie gloom.

He put on the interior light and its thin yellow glow threw shadows on his face. It was a silent dark world and the windows misted over quickly with our breath.

'I used to come here when I was a boy,' my father said. 'It's been a long day and I'm going to rest for a bit, but I've got to take a pee first, though.' He opened the car door and climbed out.

I watched as he walked a few yards away and heard a stream of urine hitting the bushes. Afterwards his back remained turned to me but I could see the red tip of a cigarette glowing in the dark. His hand went to his mouth and faintly, against the gloom, I saw the white plume of smoke curling up and swirling around his head. During the time it took for him to smoke it, his face remained hidden. When he took the last drag he threw it on the ground and slowly flattened it beneath his shoe before walking back towards me.

His face in the shadows was just a pale blur that gradually came closer until he climbed back into the car. I looked at him enquiringly and saw his eyes were dark holes, devoid of expression that, I thought then, were not looking at but through me. A knot of apprehension formed in my stomach. I knew instinctively that the months during which he had not touched me had ended, and whatever he had made me do before, this time, in this dark and desolate place, it was going to be worse.

'Get in the back, Sally,' he ordered me.

I shook my head, but even as I did so I knew it was a pointless gesture. At only eight, I was no match for him.

He made no response to the pleas and tears that came later. Instead he got out of the car again, reached across the driver's seat, grabbed my arm and, with one quick movement, pulled me out of the car and threw me face down on the long back seat. He did not utter a word as he pulled my legs until they dangled over the seat with my feet nearly touching the ground. Nor did he speak when he yanked down my knickers and woolly tights before forcing my legs apart.

I shivered as the chill of approaching night touched my bare skin. I could hear his breath rasping and my own feeble pleas – 'No! Please, Daddy, no' – but still he was silent.

I felt his hands going under my buttocks, felt the hard thing pressing against me, and heard him spit on his finger before he pushed it into me.

'You're ready for it now,' he said, the first words he had spoken since he had come back to the car.

It was then that my father raped me. In that cold forest where the light from the rising bone-white moon danced between the leaves and threw spots of light down on us.

I could smell him and the leather of the seat as my cheek pressed into it. I felt the cold air on my legs, but most of all I could feel him as he thrust into me. The rough fabric of his trousers rubbed against my legs and I heard his grunts and the creak of the car as it moved with him.

And with each thrust, each groan, each sigh and each creak, I felt the soul of my childhood shrivel and die. With it went the seeds that good nurturing sows and parental love makes grow; the seeds of conscience, kindness and the ability to love selflessly. Those seeds left me, along with my belief that adults are there to protect children. In their place there was just a space filled with need: the need for praise, the need for acceptance and the need to be loved, but the capability of returning love was gone.

That night it was not just my childhood that my father killed: he also destroyed the woman I could have become.

I can't remember what he said to me that time but I can vividly recall his words on the many other nights when he raped me. I have no reason to doubt that his words then would have been the same. Each time that he forced himself on me, they seldom varied: 'That was nice, wasn't it, Sally?' Hearing him, I would always shake my head, for in the early days, his actions rendered me incapable of speech. But my show of denial only earned me his laughter; laughter that contained no mirth.

'I know you wanted me to do that, Sally,' he would say. 'I've seen you watching me with those big cat's eyes of yours.'

How could I tell him that what I kept looking for was the old daddy? The one who I still wanted to see. It was his love I yearned for when, thinking I was unobserved, I searched his face for a smile; the one that was just for me.

I can remember all those times so clearly: the lingering memories never let me forget them. At night they visit me in my dreams until I force myself awake. Then, angrily, I wipe away the tears of a small child that dampen the face of the middle-aged woman I now am. The dreams of more than thirty years later still won't let me forget those evening halts in wooded areas and later, when Sue recommenced her girls' nights out, his visits to my pink-and-white bedroom.

I can still feel the contempt and anger he showed me, but what I cannot remember is the pain. It must have been such a searing pain that tore through my body and entered every part of me that I would have been shaking with it long after the deed was finished. But while I can see my childhood self sobbing, as slime and blood trickled down my cold legs, I can't remember it.

Oh, I can still feel the sense of violation as he entered me, almost feel his shudders as those acts ended in his groaning climaxes, and behind closed lids see, once my periods had started, the pale used condoms left on bushes or in long grass. But there's a space where that other memory should be. Perhaps, finding it unbearable, I pushed it into another part of my mind. There, my dark memory slid it into a tiny box and, in my fear that one day it might escape, I slammed the lid shut, then buried it deep under other thoughts.

Every time it was over he would put his arm around my shoulders and pull me against him. That one act of tenderness turned him, my violator, into my comforter. Then the voice of the man, who as a small child I had loved, would fill my ears. As sobs shook my body, tears were wiped away and his hand stroked my back as he soothed me.

'Shush, Sally, shush,' he would murmur, until my cries subsided. 'This is what daddies do to little girls they love. It's teaching them to become women. Stop crying. You're a big girl now.' But once I had stopped, his voice would change and its flat, scornful tones showed his contempt for me. Then he would push me away.

'Anyhow, I know you wanted it,' was one of his often repeated accusations.

'I didn't,' I would gasp.

'Well, you'll soon learn to like it,' he told me firmly.

I knew I wouldn't. But each time it happened I still leant against him when his hand stroked me and his voice whispered those soothing words.

Once I was calm again he would give me a cloth he kept in the glove compartment, if we were in the car, or hand me a tissue if we were in my bedroom. 'Here, clean your-self with that.' And each time I obediently did, before pulling my knickers back on.

'Sally,' he said repeatedly, 'this is something special be-tween us. You mustn't talk about it, do you understand?'

'Yes,' I replied, when I was eight, nine and ten. After that, when I no longer believed him any more, it was too late: by my own actions I had been labelled a liar and had created a world in which he was safe from anything I could have said.

But until then I listened to the subtle threats of being taken away and heard his promises that, as long as I was good, he would never let it happen.

Then there was the other threat that frightened me even more – one he didn't need to voice again: if I didn't obey him I would spend eternity in hell and never see my mother again.

'I won't tell,' I said.

'Let's get you home' – or, if he had visited my room, 'Go to sleep now,' said in a calm voice as though nothing untoward had happened.

Often, the next day, there would be a present for me of packets of sweets or chocolate. 'For my special girl,' he would say, and each time I would see the resentment on Sue's face.

'You spoil her,' she said accusingly. But he took no notice.

Chapter Forty-five

After the death of my mother, when our old house had become a cold, unhappy place there had been little supervision, but the new one was run strictly, according to Sue's rules. She saw it as her domain. After all, as she pointed out to my father during their rows, it was her family who had bought it, and him and his children who benefited from it.

Any sign of Dolly's presence had to be cleared from the garden the moment I arrived back from school. Outside the back door there was a trowel and plastic bags. Before I was allowed to enter the house I had to search the lawn. I bent double with my head down, scared that if I missed anything there would be another argument about getting rid of my little dog.

Shoes were taken off before entering the house, all toys had to be kept in our rooms, homework had to be done upstairs and there was no question of Dolly being allowed further than the kitchen. Within weeks of our moving in, Sue's half-hearted courtship of Billy's and my affection ceased. The attraction of a ready-made family had vanished and he and I were pushed aside. I had heard the saying that children should be seen and not heard, but Sue didn't want either.

If I sat in the lounge with a book I was told to take it upstairs. If I asked to watch anything on television she said it was bad for me, and if I went into the kitchen when she was preparing food she told me I was in the way.

Then I would creep into the garden to play with Dolly or take her for short walks, with Billy trotting along beside me. 'Don't go far,' was always Sue's warning when we left. Apart from issuing instructions or reprimands, she had little to say to us.

She had stopped working at her father's firm soon after the move. 'Got enough to do looking after the house and your children,' I heard her say.

Billy and I started at the local school and now it was my turn to take a younger family member with me each morning. To begin with I liked my new school. Gold stars were given out for my work and, eager to earn more, I would sit in my room with my school books propped in front of me, diligently preparing for the next day's lessons.

Spelling was something I worked at. I would try and memorize each letter until they looked like so many black squiggles and my eyes burnt, but it was worth it the next day when the teacher praised me; and I was becoming addicted to praise.

The children at the local school, unlike my previous one, were friendly. They knew nothing about my mother, her drinking or her breakdowns, and within a few weeks of starting, I found myself being asked to parties or to visit.

But when I asked Sue's permission to go, instead of being pleased that I was being accepted by the local children, she was more concerned about who they were. An inquisition about the family and which part of the town they lived in would follow any mention of a child at school.

'I don't think so, Sally,' was Sue's answer, when I told her the name of each new friend I had made.

The excuses she gave varied. Sometimes it was because they worked for her family and therefore my father; at others she didn't approve of their address or the work their father did. When the invitation was for the weekend, there would be a sigh. 'No, not this time, Sally. There's no one to take you and bring you back. Your father works hard all week so we're not going to ask him, are we?'

Once I asked if I could have a friend over to visit me, but my request was met with a horrified look. 'No, Sally. I have quite enough to do feeding and cleaning up after you and Billy, without having more children in the house. Your father needs his rest after work – he doesn't want noisy children running around.'

The sound of Dolly welcoming me on my return from school would bring Sue rushing to the door. Her face would scrunch up in exasperation when she saw the little dog yapping excitedly as, tail wagging, she jumped up to greet me. 'Sally, keep that dog quiet! We don't want to upset the neighbours, do we?'

Billy, once chubby and lively, now looked despondent. Used to being fussed over by my grandmother and my aunt, he pined for his old home and the people who had brought him up since my mother had died. 'Want Nana,' he would say repeatedly, and his language became more babyish again. He started sucking his thumb, which infuriated Sue. 'It's unhygienic and looks terrible. Take it out of your mouth now,' she would shout at him.

Toys that were noisy, such as the drum he had been given by my aunt, were confiscated and games of hide and seek or any of the others we had played together were now forbidden. She had refused to allow him to bring my old Space Hopper, which he loved, to the new house.

'Don't want that scuffing up the lawn,' she had said, when he didn't want to part with it. The lovely new things that Sue had promised the house would be full of had not included toys. He was at an age when little boys find it difficult to be quiet, and now that he had no cousins to play with, he became bored and depressed. At five his baby plumpness faded and his wide, trusting smile disappeared. Sue might have turned him into a well-behaved child, but she had not created a happy one.

She believed that I was my father's favourite and knew that I was old enough to tell him if she ever raised her hand to me. However, she also seemed to know that being ignored was punishment enough for me. Billy was not so lucky, and should he forget one of her increasing number of rules or fail to respond immediately to her commands, not only did harsh words fall on him but also a stinging slap.

Before and after my grandfather's death, Sue steadfastly found excuses not to visit my father's family. A dinner party, an invitation to her parents', or a visit to one of her friends always took precedence over any proposed visit to her in-laws. At weekends she decided what she and my father would do, especially if there were powerful people she wanted to impress. Then Billy and I were shown off and banished to our rooms.

'Oh, Sue,' I heard a female friend say to her, 'I do think you're brave taking on another woman's children like you have.'

'Oh,' she said airily, 'it's no trouble and they're so sweet.'

Sue's rules increased to our detriment. Family meals on Saturday evenings came to an abrupt stop. 'I think it's better if you and Billy eat together on Saturdays,' she told me. 'Then afterwards you can go to your rooms and play.' She bought a small television and installed it in my room. 'You can watch it up here,' she said brightly. 'Look how lucky you are – your own TV.' It was followed by a cassette player and some of the latest cassettes.

'When we have visitors, Dolly can go up to your room until they leave,' she told me, as an extra bribe.

'The children have already eaten,' she told my father, when he looked puzzled to see the dining-table set with just two places. Billy and I had been given tinned macaroni cheese in the kitchen for our supper, and my mouth watered at the aroma of meat simmering in red wine that was wafting throughout the house.

'David, we have to have our privacy,' she said the next weekend, when she had ordered me to take Billy and go to my room while it was still light. 'Sally's room has everything she could possibly want and I've even let her take that dog of hers upstairs for company too. We need some "us" time, don't we, darling?' she said sweetly.

She was right: my room did have everything in it a girl could want. The only problem was that, apart from Billy and Dolly, there was nobody to enjoy it with me. Billy was too young to sit still for long and he irritated me when he fidgeted with my belongings. On the other hand he looked so miserable at the change in his circumstances that I felt too sorry for him to grumble. After the initial excitement of having a cassette player and my own television wore off, the walls of my room started to close in on me, until it felt more like a prison than a room a child could relax in.

'Sally, show Auntie So-and-so . . .' Sue would name one of her many friends, with the request to take her to my room. Up the stairs I would have to go with whoever it was and show them everything that Sue had put into it.

'Well, aren't you a lucky girl?' was always the response, followed by praise for Sue.

'Don't spoil them too much,' the 'auntie' would always warn Sue, when she returned to the lounge. Then, with Billy following me, I would go back upstairs.

Chapter Forty-six

Over the next few months my father and I drove down to visit my grandmother three times, and three times he stopped the car in the woods on the return journey.

'Why will you not take Billy as well?' Sue asked petulantly – a day with no one else in the house meant a day of bathing in scented warm water, painting her nails and covering her face with a mud pack. 'I wanted to go to the hairdresser's,' she said crossly, on the third visit. 'I didn't marry you to be your children's babysitter.'

More rows followed, but she had her way and Billy came too during the Easter holidays. After that, apart from when he was ill with mumps or measles, he came with us on each visit, much to the delight of Nana and my aunt, but most of all me. Unknowingly, he had become the chaperone who kept me safe.

It was then that Sue, angry about my father's long days away from her, resumed her nights out with the girls – Her 'me time' or 'catch-up time'. 'I need them, David,' she said. But I noticed that she didn't seem very pleased when he failed to protest.

It was on a night when Sue was at one of her weekly girls' nights out that my father let me know just how much power he had over me.

I was nearly ten. Unable to engineer any time with me

when we were completely on our own, my father had left me alone for some time. Sue's night out gave him the opportunity he had been waiting for. Safe in the knowledge that she wouldn't return until late and that Billy was asleep, he risked coming into my room.

I was reading with the bedside light on when I heard my door open and looked up to see him standing there. 'Hello, Sally,' he said. 'It's been a long time since we were alone together, hasn't it?' Pulling the bedclothes right up to my chin, I looked fearfully at him over the top of my pink quilt.

His mouth was twisted into the conspiratorial smile I recognized while his eyes raked the outline of my body. 'Stop hiding under the bedclothes – I know you want it. A dirty little girl like you always does.'

'I don't,' I whispered, gripping the covers as though they afforded me some protection.

'Sally, what have you been told about lying? You get punished for it, don't you?'

I looked at him, not understanding what he meant but knowing that something bad was going to happen.

He moved fast, taking me by surprise. With strong fingers, he grasped my shoulders and pulled me out from under the blankets. Then, grabbing one of my pillows, he flung me on to my back and pressed it over my face.

I felt the weight of him pushing me down; my chest tightened and I could hear my blood drumming in my ears. My legs kicked out, but my arms were trapped by the quilt and blankets as I tried to reach out to his hands. But I was powerless to move and the feeble twists of my small body did nothing to dislodge the pillow, which was suffocating me.

It must have been just a few seconds, but in my panic it felt like hours before he released me. When he lifted the pillow, I still couldn't breathe. My chest burnt, black dots danced in front of my eyes and my breath came in rasping gasps as I tried in vain to get air into my lungs. I looked at him imploringly. I needed my inhaler. Since I had my first asthma attack I was frightened of being anywhere where I couldn't get to my medication. The attacks now happened regularly and it was only when I held it in my hand and was ready to place it on my mouth that my panic, which increased the ferocity of the attacks, ceased.

Although I was now allowed to carry it to school, in the house it was either Sue or my father who had control of it.

'But what happens if I need it in the night?' I had asked fearfully, when my father told me they were keeping it in their room. 'What happens if I can't call you or you don't hear me?'

My father told me I was being over-dramatic: of course I could call out or knock on their door. Asthma didn't paralyse me, did it? And using the inhaler too much was dangerous – hadn't the doctor told me so?

But that night I needed it and it was only my father who had the power to give it to me. He stood watching me, as I tried to get my breath. Eyes wide with panic, I saw he was holding it in his hand. 'Is this what you want, Sally?' he asked, and frantically I stretched my hand out to take it. He laughed and took a step backwards so it was out of my reach. 'Say "please", Sally.' Still my breath rasped in my throat and I couldn't get the word out. My chest tightened even more and still I could see him smiling at me as he taunted me with my inhaler.

'What? Can't speak?' He let me see it dangling from his hand.

'Please,' I managed to gasp out between coughs.

'That's better,' he said, and held it out to me.

I grabbed it, put it to my lips and felt the release of pressure as I puffed it into my mouth. Gradually my breathing eased and I puffed again.

'Enough, Sally,' he said, and took it back.

Weakly I lay on the bed. The pillow that had been over my face was now behind my head. I felt my body going hot and cold. My face was beaded with sweat and tears and my pyjamas clung damply to me.

He left the room and came back holding a damp face-cloth and a glass of milk. He wiped my face gently, then wrapped my fingers round the glass. 'Drink this. It'll make you feel better,' he said, in his nice-daddy voice. Gratefully, I swallowed it.

'There,' he said tenderly. 'Daddy's made it all better. What do you say, Sally?'

'Thank you,' I answered, knowing the game wasn't over.

'Now admit you want me,' he said, and seeing that I was looking at him numbly, his hand snaked out towards my bedside table where he had placed the inhaler. 'Say it, Sally.'

Terrified that he would do the same thing again, I said the words he wanted to hear. 'Yes,' I whispered, and felt the bed sag with the weight of his body as he climbed in beside me.

Chapter Forty-seven

It was after that night that I started creating a secret world in my head, an imaginary place where I could take myself when reality became too cruel, a world in which my mother was still alive, and it was to her that I talked.

I had forgotten that when she was alive she had failed to keep me safe from my father. In my new world that was why she had sent me away: her knowledge of what he was like was in the story she had told me. He was the dragon, wasn't he? And the people who had taken in the little girl were my aunt and uncle. But, of course, the little girl hadn't lived happily ever after with them. My mother had died not knowing that.

At night as I slipped into sleep, it was my mother I confided in. I told her of my fears and in my mind she comforted me.

I withdrew from my classmates – what did I have by way of interesting conversation that would amuse them? I felt very remote as I watched groups of girls giggling in the playground. They talked of family outings – we didn't have any; of playing at each other's houses and parties – I wasn't allowed to do or go to either. Having issued invitations that had always been refused, they now saw my remoteness as unfriendliness. Gradually they stopped trying to include me in their games, and invitations to their homes ceased.

My mind was constantly full of my mother and I wanted her back in my world so much that it hurt. In my imagination I had taken the person I had loved, eradicated from my memory her bad days and turned her into the perfect mother. Hopes, dreams and far-fetched wishes became fantasies that I turned into endless stories with myself as the heroine, then replayed them, like films, over and over again in my mind.

Sometimes I was a famous pop star standing in front of a crowd of adoring fans, or an athlete winning at sports with the whole school applauding, or surrounded by friends who listened to my every word. And in every dream my complexion was clear and I could breathe without fear of asthma. Gradually the dream world in my head became more and more real until fact and fantasy were completely intertwined and I frequently retreated into it.

As my imagination ran unchecked, I brought my mother back to life. I began to believe that she had run away and was hiding from my father; not me – never me – but always him. Had he made her do the same things that hurt me? I wondered if that was why she had left us. I started to see her in strange places but she was always just out of my reach. In the streets I often thought I'd spotted her but she was always in the distance. I saw the whirl of a bright, flowing skirt, a cloud of long blonde hair and opened my mouth to call her. But before I did, I realized it was a stranger who resembled her.

That was the first part of the story I made up – part fantasy, part wish. And when I had convinced myself it was true, I told the other girls in my class. 'My mummy's not really dead,' I told them. 'She's in hiding, but she's coming back soon.'

My classmates looked at me disbelievingly. But they were nice little girls who, on telling their mothers what I'd said, were instructed to be kind. 'It's not easy losing your mother when you're a little girl,' they were told, something that was repeated to me later. As those stories were harmless, nobody told the headmistress or my father. It was a little later that that came about.

Chapter Forty-eight

It was on a rare occasion when I was left alone in the house that my curiosity became too much for me. I crept out of my room and went down the landing to Sue and my father's bedroom. I pushed open the door and, for a few seconds, just stood looking inside. All thoughts of the rules about going into their room were forgotten, as was the rule that I must never touch any of Sue's things: I had fastened my eyes on the dressing-table. The assortment of makeup and beauty paraphernalia on it proved too much for me to resist. My feet, almost as though they had a will of their own, took me over the cream carpet until I found myself sitting on her white-and-gold chair in front of the mirror.

I saw my child's face reflected back. Blonde hair that was still cut to just below my ears, a pale face where the last of the plumpness of youth still remained and large green eyes with thick light lashes. What would I look like wearing makeup? Sue wasn't often seen without it, but when she was, I had noticed how different she looked. Eyes that with cosmetic help seemed large and sparkling were small and nondescript with sparse lashes. When bare, her skin was rather pallid and her bone structure ill defined; the items on her dressing-table gave her high cheekbones. Her mouth was small and her lips narrow without the gleaming pale pink lipstick and enlarging outline in a darker shade. Without the help of cosmetics she was rather plain.

Slowly, one by one, I picked up the small jars, unscrewed the lids and inhaled the scent that floated out to me. A finger dipped into one came out covered with beige foundation. Before I knew it I was spreading the pale cream across my face. Another pot revealed a light orange powder for the cheeks and I brushed some on. I spat on the block of mascara, as I had watched her do at the breakfast table, and with the small brush, I started coating my lashes with a wobbly hand. I managed to smudge it on my cheeks, as I did the eye-shadow I put on next with my finger.

So intent had I been on my transformation that I hadn't heard the front door opening, or Sue's footsteps on the stairs. It was only when I heard her voice behind me that I realized she was in the room. 'Sally, what the hell do you think you're doing?' she screamed.

I cringed away from her. 'I was just trying to look pretty,' I said.

'Well, don't bother,' was her short answer. 'With those spots you're never going to be. Now go and wash it off.'

I slunk out of her room and went to the bathroom. There, I stared again at the person reflected in the mirror. My face, with its bright red cheeks, smudges of mascara and blue-stained eyelids, looked back at me with a serious expression. No, I thought. She's right. I'm never going to be pretty. I picked up the flannel and slowly wiped every trace of the makeup off my face.

Sue decided that at weekends and during the approaching school holidays I should have a friend to play with. She announced that she had chosen the perfect companion for me. 'It'll get you out of the house and give you something to do,' she said. She meant, I decided, that it would get me out of her way.

'Who is she?' I asked. I was told that her name was Jennifer and that she was the same age as me. After further questioning I learnt that she was the daughter of one of Sue's friends who, because she was a weekly boarder at an exclusive school some miles away, didn't know any of the local children. Jennifer had two older brothers who had little interest in playing with a younger sister.

Remembering how indifferent Pete had been to me when I was younger I felt something approaching sympathy for her.

'She's the right sort of girl for you to make friends with,' Sue kept telling me.

I felt a spurt of anger at her assumption that I had no other friends, which I had never admitted to her. Pride made me protest that there were other girls I wanted to visit during the holidays.

'And,' she added, by way of a bribe, 'her mother said you can take Dolly with you.'

The bribe worked.

On the appointed morning I brushed the little dog's fur, then placed her red leather collar around her woolly neck. I gave her a hug and whispered the day's plans into her fluffy ears. She licked me enthusiastically and bounced up to the car. Sue drove us to the outskirts of town, near to where her parents' house was; this was where Jennifer's family lived.

On arrival I saw a house very similar to the one that Sue

had grown up in: a large red-brick edifice that sat in the middle of what appeared to be acres of manicured lawn, surrounded by a small forest of tall trees. Plenty of room for Dolly to run around, I thought. As that idea came into my head so did another: it was likely that Sue wanted to be friendly with the wealthy family who lived here rather than her worries about my isolation.

That first day it was Jennifer's mother, a woman a decade or so older than Sue, who opened the majestic front door. I was instructed to call her 'Auntie Ann' and she looked impeccable. Her dark brown hair was cut into a gleaming bob and swung smoothly against her cheeks. Her face, with its small neat features and large brown eyes, was discreetly made up, and her pale blue linen dress, which Sue told me later was the latest Country Casuals design, looked as though it had just been ironed. Telling me that Jennifer was looking forward to my visit, she ushered us both into a room – three of its walls and the ceiling were made of glass; she referred to it as the conservatory. It was furnished with white wicker chairs that had pink-and-white-striped cushions, and on various tall stone stands there were masses of pink and white flowering plants. I heard Sue admiring it but it looked to me a lot like my late grandfather's greenhouse. Only this room was much bigger and smarter and, unlike my grandfather's with his tomatoes, none of the plants looked remotely suitable for eating.

Jennifer was already in there when we entered, and my first impression was of a plump little girl with a round, babyish face. She wore yellow cotton shorts and her feet were tucked into spotless white tennis shoes. Like mine, her hair, which was a mousy brown, was cut to just beneath her ears and kept in place with a brown hairslide.

Struck shy by the curious adults, neither of us wanted to say the first word and we looked at each other warily. It was Dolly that broke the ice. Within seconds of seeing my little dog, Jennifer was down on the floor stroking her.

'Don't let her lick your face,' I heard her mother say to Jennifer before she turned to Sue: 'Dear little thing, isn't she?'

I was amazed to hear Sue say, 'Yes,' as though she had never thought of giving Dolly away.

A tray with a silver teapot, china cups and a plate of biscuits was brought in by a teenage girl. She was called an au pair, I found out later, and had arrived from France a few weeks earlier. She was there to improve her English, teach the children French and help with a little light housework.

Jennifer and I were given juice and biscuits before my latest auntie told her daughter to show me around while she and Sue had a 'nice little chat'. Needing no more than those few words of encouragement, Jennifer and I left the two adults and hurried out into the grounds with Dolly scampering at my side.

That day we explored the orchard, where the fruit was still too green to pick. We took turns throwing a ball for Dolly and watched with glee as the little dog sped after it as fast as her legs would carry her, returning with it in her mouth, ready for us to throw it again. After lunch, which we ate outside in the garden, we changed into swimsuits and spent the afternoon playing in the family's new swimming-pool. I had to wear blow-up armbands although Auntie Ann said the au pair could start teaching me to swim the next time I came. The pretty pool was surrounded by pink busy lizzies. Jennifer told me that her mummy had five hundred planted early each summer by the local nursery. I momentarily remembered our dusty little back garden, which my mother had been too depressed to attend to, and a shadow must have fallen over my face. Jennifer, mistaking my expression for something else, splashed me and we resumed chatting and playing in the warm water. Dolly sat on the side of the pool wagging her tail and giving the occasional bark.

By the end of the afternoon I felt Jennifer and I had become firm friends, and when Sue called to collect me, I left feeling thrilled that there was an arrangement for the following Saturday for me to visit Jennifer again.

It was, however, a friendship that was not going to last, for in the course of the next few weeks my actions would ensure its curtailment. But that day, not being able to see into the future, I believed that during the long summer holidays Dolly and I would have someone to play with.

Chapter Forty-nine

It was a Friday afternoon and I was in the kitchen, transfixed by Sue's fast-moving hand as it expertly held a small sharp knife and chopped an assortment of vegetables into tiny regularly sized squares. It was then that I noticed the bracelet she was wearing on her arm: a wide silver band trimmed with copper and, in the centre, an engraving of a long-legged bird. There was something familiar about it, and the more I looked, the more convinced I became that I had seen it before. As I searched my mind for when that could have been, a picture gradually came to me. It was of another kitchen, where a blonde woman stood at a kitchen table and a small child was watching her. I saw a mischievous smile, sparking green eyes, then heard a familiar voice that held a hint of laughter: 'I'm cooking something special for tonight's dinner, Sally,' and as her arm stretched out for the knife, the child's eyes fixed on the pretty bracelet worn around a slender wrist.

'Where did you get that bracelet?' I asked.

Surprised that I had asked her a question about anything to do with her appearance, Sue glanced up at me. 'Your father gave it to me for my birthday. Pretty, isn't it?'

I felt a white-hot anger send a rising heat through my body and it pinked my cheeks. How could my mother's bracelet be on Sue's arm? 'It was my mother's,' I yelled indignantly.

Sue's face went dark with anger and she snapped, 'Don't be ridiculous, Sally – how could it have been? Your father bought it at the local jeweller's.'

But I saw doubt cross her face as she said it. 'I should have it, not you!' I spat furiously.

'That's enough of this ridiculous nonsense, Sally!' Sue screamed. 'Now go to your room!'

Furious at seeing something that had once belonged to my mother on Sue, I slammed the door behind me on the way out of the kitchen. When my father returned from work I crept to the top of the stairs and heard Sue telling my father about my accusation. 'If it was hers I don't want it, David,' I heard her say, and then came the deeper tones of my father's voice as he fervently denied it.

By the end of their argument both of them were angry with me, my father because I'd caused trouble and Sue because I'd made her doubt him, and for the rest of the evening I was ordered to remain in my room. My supper was put on a tray, which Sue gave to me with instructions that I was to stay where I was. Hurt and angry I retreated into another fantasy, which had already started to germinate in my head.

In the morning I sat sullenly at the table, pushing my breakfast around my plate. 'It was Mummy's,' I said defiantly, when my father told me he never wanted to hear me mention the bracelet again.

'That's quite enough, Sally,' he roared, echoing Sue's words from the night before. 'Now get yourself off to school.'

Still angry, I snatched up my satchel and, with Billy

trailing miserably behind me, left the house. I hated both of them more with every step I took. I wanted my father to leave me alone and for Sue to disappear from my life. I wondered if they were angry enough to send me back to my grandmother's or even to let me live with Aunt Janet. But I knew that was never going to happen: although I was convinced Sue would like to see the back of me, I was only too aware that my father wouldn't let me go.

Billy, not understanding what was happening, was upset by the shouting and thick atmosphere in the house and walked quietly by my side. Once we got to school, he was pleased to escape my self-absorbed company and disappeared into a group of small children the moment we walked through the gates.

All day I brooded on what I could do to hurt them and then an idea came into my head. Sue, with her passion for detective books, had a collection that was scattered around the house. Without her knowing I had smuggled them up to my room and devoured the bloodthirsty stories. I read wide-eyed about dead bodies found in woods, others discovered floating in dank rivers or buried in out-of-the-way places. The murder weapons were mainly guns, knives or ropes, but there had been a couple I had read in which the cause of death had been poison, always given in tiny doses over a lengthy period of time. The motive for the murders seldom varied: they were for financial gain or love and in some cases both.

The one I recalled most clearly was where a man wanted his wife's life-insurance money and the freedom to marry his mistress so he had gradually poisoned his wife. He had thought that the small doses he had administered over several months would be undetectable, but he had not taken into consideration the cleverness of the detective who finally unmasked him. I decided that was exactly what had happened to my mother. My imagination was in full flight as I remembered Pete telling me that my father had known Sue long before my mother had died. And hadn't my mother's death benefited him? I compared the home we had now to the shabby council house we had lived in before.

Over the next few days, fuelled by rage, hurt and the desire to make it true, I embroidered my fantasy until it took shape and grew and I began to believe it. That was why I had been sent away to Aunt Janet's, I decided, ignoring the fact that it was my mother not my father who had arranged for me to go there. Neither did I take into account that I had been only six, too young to notice very much. It was Pete who had stayed in the house and, as a teenager, would have known what was wrong with my mother. But there was no logic to my reasoning, just a growing desire for it to be true.

For nearly a week I kept my thoughts to myself. But I hugged that fantasy and embellished it. I was waiting for the right moment to share it with others.

Chapter Fifty

The day after I'd talked about the bracelet to my father was Saturday and I wondered if, as a punishment, Sue would stop me going to Jennifer's. To my relief, she said nothing about it when she saw me in the morning. I took that to mean that the subject was closed, if not forgotten. And I saw with a burst of satisfaction that the bracelet was not on her arm. After I had eaten my breakfast I put on Dolly's lead and walked the mile to where Jennifer lived. It was just over a week before school was due to break up for the summer holidays, and we had been talking about things we wanted to do during those six weeks.

For the first time I met Jennifer's brothers. Like her, they were at boarding-school but theirs had already broken up for the summer. They were in the orchard when we found them. Two tow-headed boys, they were standing side by side holding miniatures of my father's hard thing. At our arrival, instead of making an effort to cover themselves up, they turned their heads to look at us.

'What are they doing?' I asked, before a red-faced Jennifer could drag me away.

Hearing my question, the older one nudged his brother and laughed. 'We're having a peeing competition,' he yelled. 'Do you want to join in? Let's see if a girl can hit that tree.'

'Come on, Sally, please don't take any notice of them.

They're rude,' said Jennifer, trying to grab my hand to pull me away.

'Scaredy cats,' yelled the younger boy.

But I was no scaredy cat and I wasn't having two boys telling me I was.

'Sally, please don't,' Jennifer started to say, but I was determined to rise to their challenge. I wanted to wipe the smirks off their faces and see them replaced with admiration.

I walked over to them, taking no notice of those miniature hard things. Off came my knickers, and I confidently lifted my skirt just high enough to take aim – but not so high that they would see my private place. I leant back and forced out a trickle of fluid. But far from hitting the tree, it splashed on to my socks. Mocking jeers rang out as the two boys convulsed with laughter and pointed at my damp legs. 'See! Girls can't do it,' they hooted in unison.

'Sally, put your knickers on,' whispered Jennifer, shocked.

Her face was red with embarrassment. I suddenly felt ashamed and did as she said.

If I was embarrassed then, I was even more so when the two boys joined us in the garden at lunchtime. Sideways looks and knowing smiles were thrown in my direction and I wanted the earth to swallow me up. Why had I done that? I kept asking myself. Jennifer, noticing my discomfort, took me away from the table as soon as she could. 'Let's go to my room,' she said. 'I'll show you my new doll.'

She led me up the stairs to a large bedroom that, with its predominantly pink-and-white furniture and bedcover, was not dissimilar to the one I slept in. She showed me her collection of dolls and I spotted a row of Barbies in an assortment of different outfits on a shelf, but it was to another one, seated on a wicker chair, that she pointed. I thought she was a little old to be so enthusiastic about dolls but I pretended to be as interested in them as she obviously was.

'This is my absolute favourite,' she said. I had to admit it was a beautiful doll, the size of a small baby with golden curls, blue eyes that opened and shut, and a long white dress. 'Her name is Penelope,' Jennifer continued proudly, and showed me that underneath the dress were lacy knickers and a tiny vest.

'Let's change her clothes,' Jennifer said, as she pulled the white dress off the doll. 'Find something you think she would like to wear.' She pointed at a box filled with small dresses, nightclothes, miniature shoes, handbags and even swimwear for the assortment of dolls that adorned her room.

It was then that I asked Jennifer the question that had been burning inside me; the one I desperately wanted an answer to. She's my friend, I thought. She'll tell me the truth.

'Does your daddy ever touch you there?' I asked, and placed my finger on the part of the doll that was between its legs. I wanted to tell her that mine did and confess that I didn't like it. He had told me that was what daddies did to little girls and I wanted to know, if Jennifer's answer was yes, if it hurt and frightened her as well. I needed to know if it was all lies, and if it was, then it must be my fault that it was happening to me. All those other questions spun in my head but I just waited for her answer.

Her eyes went very round, a look of disgust replaced the smile she had worn and she slowly shook her head, as though she couldn't believe the words that had come out of my mouth.

'You're talking dirty,' she said at last. 'You're not my friend any more.'

That was when I knew without any doubt that my father had lied. She turned away from me and, unhappily, I left her, still staring down at the undressed doll.

I called softly to Dolly and crept out of the house – I didn't want her mother to ask me why I was leaving so early. Neither did I want her to see the tears that were forming in my eyes.

Jennifer had been my only friend and now I knew she no longer was.

Jennifer's mother rang Sue to say that her daughter no longer wanted to play with me. She didn't tell Sue what I had said for evidently Jennifer had refused to tell her, but she had told her mother about me taking my knickers off.

It was also unfortunate that her telephone call was the second that Sue had received that day concerning my behaviour.

Chapter Fifty-one

By Monday morning I could no longer keep the story of my mother's murder to myself. After I had left Jennifer's house so abruptly I had brooded and brooded, and over that weekend, fuelled by a combination of rage, hurt and wishful thinking, my embryonic fantasy was embroidered into something I had come to believe was true. Now I was bursting to tell someone and watch their reaction.

I waited for morning break to tell my story to the girls in my class. Gathering a group of my classmates around me, I told them I needed to take them into my confidence. 'We had to move away and come here,' I told them, 'because my father poisoned my mother.'

'I thought you said she'd left him,' one girl said, while the others gasped with pretend horror – in that community of girls, divorce and separation, let alone murder, were still rare.

'That's what I thought! That's what they told me anyway,' I replied, quickly improvising, 'but it wasn't true. They lied to me.'

Within seconds, whether they believed my story or not, the girls were clinging to my every word. I heard a collective intake of breath as, like so many sponges, they soaked up all the gory details. Questions were fired at me and that day I became adept at explaining and embellishing my creation.

I told them all about Sue, my wicked stepmother; how my father had 'carried on' with her even before my mother became ill. She had been his 'mistress', I told them, having learnt that expression from one of those clandestinely read detective books. That remark received more gasps, for even though the girls might not know what the word meant, they knew it was something shocking. I went on to describe how I had been sent away during the weeks when my mother's food was being laced with poison, omitting to mention that it was her, not my father, who had wanted me to go to my aunt Janet.

'There was a great deal of insurance money paid out to my father on my mother's death,' I told the circle of enthralled girls. I was, of course, completely unaware of whether there was any foundation of truth in this statement, but I loved the attention that my apparently informed words were creating. Carried away by the excitement of being the centre of attention, I issued accusation after accusation, each one worse and more far-fetched than the last.

It was only when the bell informed us that our break was over and we all trooped back into the classroom that the enormity of what I had done hit me. I began to feel a cold fear of the consequences. I asked myself what would happen if the girls talked and if the story got back to Sue or, even worse, my father.

I was soon to find out. No matter that I tried to corner each of my classmates and beg them to keep quiet. No matter that I said if they talked and Sue and my father found out, they might poison me as well. My story had been too sensational for them not to talk about it.

Within two days worried parents had contacted the headmistress and she fetched me from the class. 'Bring your satchel and anything of yours in your desk and come to my office,' she said. My classmates watched agog as I gathered my things and she led me from the room. I had a sinking feeling of dread with each footstep I took down the long school corridor towards her office.

She had, she told me, notified Sue of my accusations. In turn, my stepmother had contacted my father at work. They were both on their way to see her.

Sue and my father must have arrived simultaneously because they were ushered into the office together. Terrified at what their reaction might be, I couldn't look at them, and the headmistress immediately took control of the situation.

My mother's death had clearly disturbed me, she said, not unkindly. She went on to say that I had upset the other children with my stories and therefore she had to take things further.

I was to go home with Sue and my father and she said it was better if I stayed away from school until it was decided what to do with me.

I was only present for part of the interview. Then I was sent to wait on the bench outside her office in the echoing deserted corridor. I sat as close to the door as possible, trying to hear what was happening, but my sharp little ears, accustomed to eavesdropping at home, were only able to pick up some of the conversation.

Being sent away just before my mother's death must have disturbed me and fuelled the overactive imagination of a young child more than anyone had thought, my headmistress said. She asked if I had attended the funeral, and when my father said, 'No, she was at my sister-in-law's when my wife was dying,' she explained that perhaps that had been unwise. Clearly, I had not been able to accept her death. Her comments received murmurs of agreement from both adults.

I heard her say the word 'therapy', and then my father's raised voice protesting it wasn't necessary filtered through the shut door. 'No,' he told her. 'She's been in trouble before for making up stories. When my wife died, her grandmother spoilt her and now she rebels against any sort of discipline.'

I felt a flash of anger: I had never been in trouble before. Why had he lied about me to the headmistress and Sue? I heard more conversation between the three of them but I could not make out the words until my father's voice rang out clearly again. 'This fabrication has just been done to upset her stepmother, who has done nothing but try and make a nice home for her.'

More conversation and I could hear Sue's high-pitched voice again, then the firm tones of my father, 'I'll deal with it, Headmistress,' as they were seen to her door.

Then my father and Sue came out of the office and I was ordered to pick up my things and, shuffling my feet and with my head held low, I reluctantly followed them outside.

'You can go back in Sue's car,' I was told by my seething father. 'I'll deal with you later, Sally. In the meantime I have to get back to work.' Slamming the door of his car, he drove off. Too frightened to speak, I climbed into Sue's Mini, and for the short journey home she refused to say one word to me.

'I don't know what to do with you, Sally,' she said, once we were indoors. 'I know you've always resented me, but these terrible stories are just too much. We'll just have to wait until your father comes home and see what he plans to do about it.' I went to my room and miserably sat on my bed. I tried to read but as I turned the pages of my book, none of the words made any sense. I thought about what I had done and my stupidity for allowing my lies to project me into this situation. I knew I would be the laughing stock of the school and, worst of all, I feared my father's wrath.

To my surprise, my father said little about it on his return – but, then, he was skilled at biding his time. For the rest of that week I was confined to my room for most of the time and, as a punishment, my television and cassette player were removed. I was told I could read if I needed to entertain myself. But the seeming calm was only a prelude to the storm that was sure to come. I knew that my father was not going to let me get away with what I had done.

It was not until Sue's girls' night out that I understood just what a far-reaching effect those stories would have on me.

Chapter Fifty-two

I had not heard the stealthy footsteps outside in the corridor or the creak of my bedroom door opening. It was not until he had crept across the room to stand over my bed that I became aware of his presence. He leant over me until he was so close I could smell his breath. It was hot and rancid, and the feel of it on my face made the hairs on the back of my neck rise. It was the smell of stale beer and sweat, but there was something indescribable too: the scent of danger. It was as though his rage had its own potent odour that seeped out through his pores to pollute my room. My spine went cold and my fingers grasped the side of the bed in terror.

My whole body was consumed with fear; the type of fear that almost paralyses you. I held my breath and felt my legs start trembling and my stomach churning acid. My dread of what was to come completely stifled my usual pleas; it stopped me telling him I hadn't meant any harm and that I couldn't bear to be touched. But even as those thoughts entered my head, I knew that whatever I could have said would be useless.

His fingers gripped my head, forcing me to turn my face towards him, but still he hadn't spoken and his silence terrified me. I kept my eyes shut tight as though in some childish belief that my inability to see him would also render me invisible. But when he finally spoke there was nothing I could do to block out the sound of his voice. I could hear the hiss of each syllable that slid from a mouth that I knew, without looking, was twisted in fury.

'I know all about the stories you've been making up, Sally, and we need to deal with it, don't we, just you and I?' he said. 'Open your eyes and look at me,' he ordered, but still I kept them firmly shut. It was the white-hot pain that seared my scalp that forced them to fly open. When he had crept up to my bed my father had coiled thick strands of my hair around his fist and it was his tugging sharply on them that caused my agony. Tears almost blinded me and a whimper forced itself from my throat, which had gone dry with fear.

'What's the matter, Sally?' he asked mockingly, as he pulled even harder. 'Cat got your tongue, has it? Don't you want to talk about it now?' Through the film of tears I could see my father's face glaring down at me.

Summoning up every ounce of courage in my small body I tried to stand up to him. 'I know you told me lies. Other daddies don't do what you do to me – I've found out!' I said, between sobs.

Even then I wanted him to stop being terrifying, to say something nice, to tell me I was forgiven. But he didn't.

That same jeering laugh was the only response I got to my accusation. 'Is that right, Sally? So what are you going to do about it, eh?'

Another tug on my hair sent the pain rushing to every nerve ending and I imagined it coming away from my scalp in clumps. 'If you hurt me again, Daddy, I'll tell – I'll tell them what you do to me,' I said desperately.

'And who would believe you?' he sneered. 'Everyone knows you make up stories, Sally. Nobody will believe you now.' And this time his sniggers sent a chilling message that frightened me even more than his anger and his ability to cause me such pain.

'Do you know what'll happen if you say anything else about Sue and me?' I didn't answer him, for I had no idea.

'They'll take you away. They'll put you in a place like the one your mother was in. They'll say you're as mad as she was and lock you up. You remember where she was, don't you, Sally? You went there, didn't you, to that hospital ward with all those mad people? Mind you, maybe you are as mad as she was – always crying, aren't you?'

I only had a dim memory of the place my mother had been in and, knowing that, he was able to colour in the faint images I had tried so hard to forget. And colour them in he did, with graphic words that painted the wards full of sad people, with staring eyes, and cruel, bad-tempered nurses, who wore jangling keys around their waists. As he vividly described his version of that ward I was terrified of what might happen to me. 'There were other rooms in there,' he said, 'where they shot electricity into people's brains. They did it to your mother and they do it to people who make up stories,' he said, as he gave my hair another violent tug.

His other hand went round my throat and his fingers squeezed. I desperately tried to suck in air as his grip tightened. I was petrified that what had happened before when he placed the pillow over my face would happen again. My breath rasped in my chest and my whole body shook.

I reached out my hands to clutch at his as I tried in vain to break his iron grasp.

His face showed little expression as he continued to apply pressure and look down at me. Then, with a snort of something that sounded like disgust, he removed his hand from my throat but kept the other tangled in my hair.

My bedclothes were ripped off the bed and my pyjama bottoms were roughly yanked down. Using his knee, he forced my legs apart.

'No, please don't,' I gasped, but to no avail. His response was another hard yank on my hair.

'I'll do that every time you make a noise,' he spat. 'Now turn over. I don't want to look at you.' It was over in seconds. My face was pressed into the pillow and my bottom was in the air. After his bellowing climax he rolled off me, having swiftly completed an act that I was to learn over the next six years had nothing to do with love but everything to do with power and control, and the stamping of his ownership on my ten-year-old body. There was no 'Good night' in his gentler daddy's voice, just a final warning: 'Don't you ever make up lies about me or Sue again. I don't think you will, will you?'

'No,' I whispered, and he left my room to return to the one he shared with his new wife.

Something inside me withered and died that night, and he knew it. He had left me lying there feeling valueless, completely worthless. The man I had thought loved me I now knew didn't. And somehow I imagined that it was my fault, that it must be something about me that made him do what he did to me. I knew without doubt that whatever emotion he had once felt for me as a little girl had now changed into something that was terrible, bitter and twisted.

Chapter Fifty-three

I didn't return to school for the week before the summer holidays began. Fearing both the answers and the possible reprisals if I asked what was going to happen to me, I stayed in my room as much as possible.

I believed that what my father had told me was true: if I talked I would just be accused of making up even more stories. Or, worse, as the enormity of my actions sank in, whoever I told would respond as Jennifer had: they would turn away in disgust and find my very presence repulsive. It would be me, not him, who would be blamed. I was certain of it. My silly fantasies, which were now viewed as blatant lies, had played into his hands and ensured my silence.

Apart from telling me that I was not to leave the house without Sue's permission, my father said nothing more to me about the trouble I had caused. But the threats he had planted in my head were never far from my mind: they terrified me and I knew he knew it. I would catch him glancing at me, a smug smile hovering on his lips, confident that my fear would ensure my compliance.

A week after I had been sent home from school in disgrace, Billy developed a severe cold. It was then that my father announced he was going to visit his mother again. Frightened of being on my own with him, I tried desperately to think of some excuse not to have to go with him.

I said I wasn't feeling well, and then that it wouldn't be fair to Nana if I passed on Billy's germs to her. Neither of these reasons sounded credible to Sue.

'Why, Sally, I thought you loved going to your grandmother's house,' she said, her tone telling me she wanted more of an explanation for my sudden unwillingness to visit Nana.

Unable to think of another reason she would believe, I just looked at the floor and, after a few moments of silence, I came up with car sickness.

'Well, you've never mentioned that before,' she said, and I sensed that she was becoming increasingly curious about my reluctance to go with my father. She didn't question me further but I saw her giving him a puzzled look.

Knowing that only an illness would now put a stop to the visit, I hoped that Billy's cold would be inflicted on me. To even up the odds I not only sat as close to him as I could, but I also dampened my vest with cold water and wore it under my pyjamas. Not even a sniffle developed.

On Saturday I was bundled into the car for the journey to Nana's. 'You can bring Dolly,' my father said, when I reluctantly came out of the house, and while I fetched her he produced a rug that he put over the back seat for her to sit on.

Disarmed by this concession and the light patter of one-sided conversation he kept up during the journey, I gradually began to relax. 'Don't worry, Sally,' he said, just before we arrived at my grandmother's house, 'I'm not going to tell her anything about your troubles. Wouldn't want to upset or worry her, would we?'

'No,' I replied, and received a wink and a warm smile in response.

It was when my father was like this that I became more confused about my situation than ever. The violent acts that happened in my bedroom and in the woods, although I knew they were not a figment of my imagination, seemed unreal, almost as though they were part of a bad dream; a dream that took place in the darkness and the sunlight chased away. With those words of understanding, he had resumed the role of 'good daddy' and I found myself giving him an answering uncertain smile.

Before my father had finished parking the car my grand-mother, her wrinkled face wreathed in smiles, had opened her front door and was standing on the doorstep. Comforting arms were wrapped around me, hugs and kisses were exchanged and I was led into the familiar warmth of her house. My aunt bustled out of the kitchen, wiping her hands on a tea-towel, and the greetings were repeated. As though by magic a fresh pot of tea and plates of home-made cake and biscuits appeared, and were placed on the small coffee-table in the front room. As I was contentedly munching a second piece of my grandmother's jam-filled sponge, she handed me a parcel: 'Something for you to enjoy over the holidays,' she said. Unwrapping my present excitedly, I was thrilled to find two books by my favourite author.

Later, more relatives arrived and two of my older cousins went with Dolly and me to the park; the same one where in another life I had gone as a little girl with my mother. There, as I swung on the swings, watched Dolly chasing her ball and chattered nineteen to the dozen to my cousins, I was able to forget my problems and, for that afternoon, was a carefree child again.

As soon as we returned to the house the first thing I noticed was the aroma of my grandmother's cooking wafting through from the kitchen. 'Lamb casserole for supper tonight – your favourite, Sally,' she told us, before sending us all to the bathroom to wash our hands. As I had so many times before, I sat shoulder to shoulder with my cousins at the crowded table as plates piled with chunks of meat and vegetables were passed round. Nana's wonderful apple pie and custard followed, conversation flowed and, as my father had promised, nothing was said about my recent behaviour.

By the time my father and I left, the food and the day's exertions had made me feel both drowsy and contented. The happiness of the day evaporated as soon as we drove away. Would he park in those woods as he had done on other times? My hands tensed into tight fists with my fingernails digging into my palms at the mere thought of what might happen. But, to my relief, he drove past the area he normally went to and instead pulled into a lay-by. There, with his arm gently resting on my shoulders, he uttered the words I still longed to hear: that I was loved, that I was still his special girl and that I must never forget it.

'I know you'll be good from now on, Sally,' he said finally, and gave me a quick hug, then started the car and drove home.

Sue was waiting for us and, studying my face, she immediately asked me if I had enjoyed myself. That time, instead of trying to rush past her and go straight to bed, I was able to grin happily at her. 'I had a really lovely day,' I said, and proudly showed her the books that I had been given.

'She was just being silly earlier, weren't you?' my father said, throwing me a glance. 'Worried I'd talk about her made-up stories and embarrass her in front of her grandmother. Isn't that right, Sally?'

'Yes,' I replied.

I saw something in Sue's watchful eyes then that, as a child, I didn't recognize. But when I bring up that memory and examine it through my adult eyes I can identify what I saw: it was relief. Perhaps Jennifer had talked, after all.

It was during that summer holiday that Sue tried to be friendlier towards me. Maybe she, like me, was bored. Not only was I barred from Jennifer's house but I was restricted to mine and, apart from taking Dolly for her walks, for which I was only given a short time, I was still not allowed to leave home.

Certainly before her marriage to my father, Sue's life had been much more varied. She had been used to working in a busy office environment, having lunches out with her girlfriends and, from what I gleaned from bits of her conversation, there had been plenty of nights out at the smarter pubs or wine bars, and parties too, which she had loved attending. Being married to an older man with children had put paid to that. On a rare moment of intimacy she told me he didn't want any more children although she longed for a baby of her own. Then, realizing that she ought not to be confiding such things in me, she quickly changed the subject.

It entered my head then that she was lonely: she had few visits from her contemporaries during the daytime. I picked up from snippets of chat that most of them had left the small town and it was only when they visited their parents, with or without their current boyfriends, that the girls' nights out were arranged; Sue seemed to live for them.

'Have to keep up with all the gossip,' she would say, on the evenings she excitedly got ready to meet them. I took that to mean that fashion was the main topic of conversation. But now I think of it, she must have yearned for the carefree company of those youthful friends. On the few times she had tried to entertain them in our home the difference in age between them and my father was apparent even to me. Gradually she restricted herself to seeing them on her girls' nights out or for the very occasional lunch when my father was at work.

The people who made up my father and Sue's social circle were all older couples between his and Sue's father's age. Although the men would stop off at the local pub for a drink after work with a friend or colleague, the women seldom did. Their socializing was mainly done at dinner parties and, in the early weeks after her marriage to my father, it had become clear that cooking was not Sue's forte.

Realizing that she was expected to put a decent meal on the table she had enrolled on a cooking course. But once she had learnt the basics, she had decided that she was still too limited in her repertoire, and went on to do a more advanced one. From the moment we had moved into the new house, she had decided to put into practice what the latest lessons had taught her.

Big shiny pots and pans appeared in the kitchen, with thick cookery books and a wide assortment of glass jars containing herbs and spices. An array of electrical equipment was purchased from John Lewis and soon a food processor, mixer, pressure cooker, steamer, pasta maker and an ice-cream machine cluttered the initially empty worktops. A pretty apron was tied around Sue's slim waist, and nearly every day she presented us with something new at mealtimes.

She wanted to prove that she was capable of being a better cook than either my grandmother or my mother had been, even though to begin with it was their type of cooking she had learnt. 'What's your favourite meal apart from cheese on toast, Sally?' she would ask repeatedly, in the early days, and I would search my mind for a dish that was neither a casserole, which she had already managed, nor a roast, which she had yet to master.

'Billy and I like your macaroni cheese dish,' I told her hopefully.

But it was not what we liked that she was interested in. 'Well, you might like that but I'm sure it's not your father's first choice.'

I searched my mind for something he had commented on. 'He likes Nana's steak and kidney pie,' I admitted.

She was soon putting flour and butter into the mixing bowl and I knew what was going to be cooked for that night's dinner.

That summer when I was confined to the house, Sue decided that her menus were becoming too repetitive again and that her cooking needed to be more adventurous. Out came the cookery books and the many recipes she had torn from glossy magazines as she sought culinary inspiration. Remembering the success of the steak and kidney pie, she looked to see what else she could do using those particular ingredients. She reasoned that if my father liked them all put together, he would enjoy the individual components served differently. For the following week every meal seemed to have one of those items in it. Steak with onions, kidneys in red wine, pies with puff pastry covering a rich, meaty filling, and suet-crusted steak puddings.

'I've made a special meal for you tonight, David,' she would tell him, as soon as he came through the door.

'Mmm, it smells nice, dear,' was his usual response, as he sniffed the air appreciatively. 'Good to have some real home cooking.' Meanwhile Billy and I longed for something simple, for although Sue's rule of us eating separately was still in force, the leftovers from each meal were served to us the following day.

When every steak and offal recipe was exhausted she turned to the cookery books once again. 'What about pork?' she asked me, as she paged thoughtfully through the books, examining the pictures that illustrated the dishes. 'Your father likes that, doesn't he?'

I remembered my grandmother's roast leg of pork with its crisp crackling and her tangy homemade apple sauce. 'Yummy – yes, we all do,' I replied, my mouth watering as I thought of the delicious leftovers I would get.

But something as simple as a roast was not what Sue had in mind. 'No point going to a cookery course to learn something that easy,' she said airily. Remembering the burnt roast potatoes, the overcooked vegetables and flat Yorkshire puddings that had resembled limp pancakes, I thought it was a shame that her course hadn't covered that skill. Nana always said doing a good roast was just a matter of getting the timing right, something that the cookery books never taught Sue. That night when my father came back from work she showed him some large batter-covered objects. 'They,' she told him proudly, 'are deep-fried pig's trotters. I should have painted their toenails,' she said, with a giggle, when my father lifted a portion of the batter to disclose what was inside. Even he blanched at the thought.

After pork done every way imaginable, except roasted, she turned her hand to lamb. 'He likes grilled chops,' I said helpfully, but received one of her disdainful sniffs at the idea of cooking something so ordinary. 'I know that, Sally, but I've cooked them for him countless times. I'll think of something different.' Out came the cookbooks again as she settled down with a cup of coffee, a pen and a notepad at the ready. Finally, after much pondering, she headed for the shops armed with a long list. Within an hour she was back, bringing in various shopping bags. 'I'm going to try out something really different tonight,' she said.

My heart sank. Something new was usually made from a part of the animal I found repulsive to look at, let alone eat.

When I asked her what it was going to be I received a secretive smile. She said it was something she hadn't attempted before but the butcher had assured her it would be delicious.

I was given the job of peeling potatoes, then shooed out of the kitchen. 'I don't want you distracting me – it's a delicate business,' she said, and told me to take the dog out for a walk.

Later, thinking that Billy and I would be fed in the kitchen that evening, I poked my head round the door only to be asked to wash up what seemed like every available pan and utensil in the kitchen. Rolling up my sleeves I washed, rinsed and stacked them until the draining-board was buried under a pile of shiny stainless steel.

'Sally,' Sue said, when I had finished, 'for a special treat I thought we'd all eat together tonight. This dish needs to be served hot.'

I looked at her with something approaching gratitude. Spending every evening in my room alone had made me both bored and depressed. Billy could watch the children's programmes in the lounge but as part of my punishment I wasn't allowed to join him.

'No point in removing your TV from your room,' Sue had said, when I protested, 'only to have you in here as well.' She did take me to the library once a week so that at least I had something to occupy myself, but there was only so much reading I could do.

I missed Jennifer and my schoolfriends. Having no one of my own age to talk to, I even welcomed helping Sue in the kitchen, even if that help consisted mainly of washing up the numerous pots and pans she used on her cooking sprees. At least it gave me something to do and the bit of conversation that passed between us was better than nothing.

I was told to wash my hands and change and bring Billy into the dining room when she called us. Wondering what culinary delight she had conjured up, and having been told she didn't need any further help, when we heard her call I took my seat next to Billy and waited to find out.

'I've made a special meal for you tonight, David,' Sue

said predictably, as he came through the door. I saw a look of suspicion cross my father's face. He had always liked plain food, and the richness of Sue's cooking was not always to his taste.

'What – a nice roast dinner?' he asked, half joking, half hoping.

'Oh, don't be silly, Davie,' she answered coyly. 'I didn't go to cookery classes to learn what any old cook can do.'

Once we were all in our places, Sue wheeled in her latest possession, the heated hostess trolley – and, dumbfounded, I stared at what was sitting in the middle of it. It was a baked sheep's head with a protruding grey flabby tongue. Its lips, through which I could see the creature's large yellow teeth, looked as though they had been drawn back in pain – almost as though it had been alive when it went into the hot oven. The top of its head had been removed and a little bunch of watercress poked out of the hole like a silly green hat.

I was transfixed by the hideousness of it, and then I noticed the animal's eyes. They were white with dark rings around them and they seemed to stare sightlessly straight at me. I heard Billy gulp back his inclination to scream, but his hand pointed waveringly at it and his body trembled.

'Oh, for heaven's sake, Billy,' Sue snapped. 'Sit still and stop making a fuss. Now, Sally, I don't want any nonsense from you either. This is a real delicacy.' She placed it in front of my father for him to carve while she opened the top of the trolley to reveal an assortment of vegetables in glass dishes.

Whatever she wanted to call it, I couldn't bear to look

at the decapitated head sitting on one of Sue's best serving plates. My father, taking no notice of Billy's and my shocked faces, picked up a carving knife and adeptly removed the tongue, which he laid at the side of the plate. He then proceeded to cut slices from the sheep's cheeks. Finally he picked up a serving spoon and scooped out some grey slush from under the watercress at the top of the head.

As a child brought up on supermarket food – meat came in plastic trays wrapped in clingfilm and milk in cartons – I had never faced the reality of where it actually came from. When I had admired animals in the fields I had not connected them with the food that was put on our plates.

'What's the matter, Sally?' Sue asked, in a deceptively sweet tone. 'You eat bacon, don't you?' She lifted up a spoon of the grey slush and placed it on my plate. 'Brains, Sally. They're really lovely,' she said, 'and they might make you smarter.' She turned to my father. 'David, please cut a piece of tongue for her – mind you, it might have been better to have cut out Sally's a few weeks ago!' She gave the annoying tinkling laugh that, since the first day I had met her, had grated on me.

From somewhere I found the strength to pick up my knife and fork and cut the meat into small pieces. I placed it in my mouth and chewed. If I didn't look at that ruined head and just thought of it as a slice of lamb, I told myself, I could get it down.

I watched Billy out of the corner of my eye. He, too, seemed to have come to the same conclusion and was manfully chomping away.

My father heaped praise on Sue for cooking such a traditional northern dish. He told her it was delicious and recalled his own grandmother serving sheep heads. 'Yours is much better, though, Sue, really it is,' he added. Billy and I managed to say we had liked it too and kept our fingers crossed that this was not going to be a regular addition to her menus.

It was after our dessert, which I thought looked like a crushed ice-lolly and she called 'sorbet', that she decided it was time to tell me what was going to happen to me once the school holidays were over.

'You're going to a new school,' my stepmother informed me. In a voice that said, 'This hurts me more than it hurts you', she added, 'One where I hope you won't make up any more stories,' thus dashing my hopes that my misdemeanour, if not forgotten, was not to be mentioned again.

'Why can't I stay at the one I'm at?' I asked, feeling panic at the idea of changing schools again. For a moment I thought she meant a boarding-school, and however bad it was at home, I knew I didn't want to go to one.

'You've upset your classmates, and their parents have complained about you. Your father and I have discussed it and think it will be better for you to have a completely fresh start,' she told me, trying to make everything seem as though it was just my best interests that she had at heart.

'Yes, Sally,' my father butted in. 'Sue's father told me that your stories were repeated to him by one of our employees. Imagine how embarrassing that was! He said that you're the talk of the town. And that's not good for business, is it, when people who are supposed to respect me are laughing about my daughter behind my back? And goodness knows what you said to Jennifer – her parents don't want you in their house again.'

I sat straighter in my chair, feeling his eyes boring into my head. I was thankful that Jennifer would be back at boarding-school in a few weeks and that our paths were unlikely to cross. If she didn't see me, then surely she would forget what I had said to her – at least, I hoped so. I didn't want to try to imagine just how terrible my punishment might be if my father ever heard what I had asked her.

He carried on as though he hadn't noticed my discomfort: 'They're friends of Sue's family, influential people, and now we can never take you to their house. Yes, you've made everything very awkward for us. Still, I'm not going to say any more about it.'

I made no comment, just stared at my empty plate.

Not wanting the awkward atmosphere to ruin her special meal, Sue decided to lighten the conversation. 'Anyhow, Sally, next week I'm taking you shopping for a new uniform – I thought we might even have some tea out,' she chimed in brightly.

Already smarting from her comments about brains and tongue, I thought sourly that she wasn't fooling me with her talk of shopping. She wanted an excuse to go into the next town, which was more than ten miles away and much larger than the one we lived in.

Chapter Fifty-four

The school was several miles from home and much larger than the local one I had attended previously. Sue pointed it out to me when she drove us to the shops. Unlike the neighbourhood one, which was housed in an old building, this school was a modern brick, steel and glass Meccano-like construction. To me, it looked a vast, soulless place and Sue's chatter that it had every modern amenity did nothing to allay my misgivings.

She parked in a multi-storey car park, then set off purposefully in the direction of the shops, with me trailing along beside her. The first stop was a store where school uniform items were sold. This time I needed a navy skirt and blazer plus a grey jumper and two white shirts. Pulling the items hurriedly off the rail, she bundled them into my arms. 'Try that one on as well,' she said, holding up a second blazer that I could see was miles too big. I protested that I thought everything was the wrong size, but it had no effect on her and I took them into the changing room. The skirt hung to mid-calf and the blazers swamped me, as did the shirts.

'They're all too big – look!' I said, as I came out of the changing room.

She sighed. 'Sally, have you any idea what this constant school changing is costing us? And you can't have a new uniform whenever you grow an inch, can you?'

I mumbled, 'No.'

'No,' she repeated. 'We don't want this expense again for a few years, so you'll just have to grow into them.'

'But I'll look stupid!'

'Well, whose fault is that?' was her tart rejoinder. As soon as I had changed back into my own clothes she handed everything to the shop assistant, saying we would take everything. My satchel, the one my mother had given me to start school with, was to be replaced with a brief-case that she also added to the pile. 'You need something bigger than that old one,' she said.

'But everyone else will have a satchel,' I tried to tell her – like all children I had a fear of looking different from my peers.

'Not everyone, Sally. You won't,' she replied, and I saw a smile of satisfaction cross her face at my dismay.

When the purchases had been packed, Sue led the way to the ground floor. There, I found out that I had been right: the shopping trip was more for her than for me. She spent about the same amount of time and almost as much money choosing makeup and beauty products as she had on selecting my uniform.

Once the spending spree was finished she turned to me with a smile. 'We're going to have some lunch now, Sally,' she said brightly. 'I need to freshen up.' We made a detour to the 'ladies restroom' as the sign said on the door. Out came the new blusher and pink lipstick, which were skil-fully applied, her hair was fluffed up and perfume sprayed on wrists and neck. With one last look in the mirror, Sue decided she was ready.

Click, click, went her stilettos as she marched briskly down the road. 'A friend's going to join us,' she told me.

Join you, I thought, but wisely said nothing.

Into a small dimly lit wine bar we went to find her friend was already there. As they greeted each other the friend's blonde bouffant hair bounced, her pale lips smiled, and the two nearly identical women air-kissed and exchanged compliments – 'You look wonderful,' and 'So do you' – while the waiter prepared to take the order.

A few brief words were said to me, before the two women settled down to chatter. Bored with their conversation about fashion and the details of the latest boyfriend, I tried to block it out. It must have been about an hour later when they looked at their watches. 'Work calls,' said the bouffant blonde, and 'Husband's dinner too,' responded a giggling Sue. More air-kisses, then we were outside and on the way to the car.

The following week the summer holidays ended and it was time for me to start at another new school. On the first day Sue drove me there. 'After today you can catch the bus,' she said, and showed me the stop where I was to find the return bus that afternoon.

When we arrived she told me that the headmaster was expecting us and led the way to his office. She greeted him warmly, then introduced me. He was a tall, thin man, with flinty eyes and sparse grey hair. He looked at me coldly through large horn-rimmed glasses when Sue informed him that I was the stepdaughter she had told him about.

'I'll leave her with you, then,' she said, giving him one of her wide flirtatious smiles. 'You be good now, Sally,' were her final words to me before she disappeared through the door, leaving me standing in my too-big uniform, facing a man who had already judged me as a potential troublemaker. I felt a sinking sensation as I heard her echoing steps receding down the hall. For all her faults, at least she was familiar.

'Well, Sally,' he said, taking his seat behind the desk but leaving me standing. 'Your stepmother and father have told me of some of your problems. Let me tell you this. That sort of behaviour will not be tolerated here. Girls who tell lies about others are punished. Do you understand me?'

My heart sank even more. This was not as I had been told – a fresh start: I had simply been removed from the local children who might repeat anything I said and cause my father and Sue embarrassment – or worse.

'Yes.'

'Yes who, Sally?'

'Yes, sir,' I said.

His face did not change expression as he continued, 'I'll be getting regular reports from your teachers and will be monitoring your progress.'

He paused then, waiting for some response, but receiving none he continued his lecture in the same dismissive tone. 'Now, as you can't do sport, you will spend those lessons studying extra English and maths in the library, so don't think you can slack off. Do you understand what I am saying?'

'Yes,' I said. He raised an eyebrow quizzically, reminding me of what he expected to hear. 'Yes, sir,' I whispered and, satisfied with my meekness, he escorted me to my classroom.

At the first break I looked nervously about as children had already formed their groups and stood around me chatting. No one looked friendly, only curious when they glanced in my direction. I saw their heads lower, heard muttering, and instinctively knew it was me they were talking about.

One boy sauntered over to where I stood and I could feel his friends watching with interest as they crowded round. 'Heard you make up stories,' he said, with a smirk.

'Yes,' chimed in another voice, which belonged to a thick-set little girl, 'and the teacher told us to tell on you if you do it here.'

I felt my face redden and tears prickled behind my eyes as I tried to say I didn't.

'You speak posh, don't you?' jeered another, but I couldn't explain that was because of the therapy I'd had to improve my speech impediment. I knew he would only laugh at me more.

At lunchtime when, with the other children from my class, I walked into the bustling canteen, no one moved to make room for me to sit so, taking my tray, I perched alone at the end of a table. All around me was the buzz of conversation, but none of it was directed at me.

It was no better at the end of the day when I was leaving.

'Hey, Sally,' yelled one of my classmates. 'Got a big sister, have you? She given you her cast-offs?'

'What's that you're carrying, then?' called another, pointing at my briefcase.

'Yeah, you're a snob, aren't you? Think you're better than us,' shouted another, and I heard hoots of derisive laughter following me as I walked to the gates. I knew then that, no matter how long I was at that school, I was never going to make friends.

Within a few days of the start of term my eczema returned in full force. Once again the rash covered my arms and crept up my neck to my face. The same words that had been hurled at me when I was five – spotty, stinky and dirty – were now repeated, but this time the children were older and injected more venom into their voices. 'Spotty-spotty Sally,' they chanted whenever the rash was visible. Wanting to escape my tormentors I would disappear into the toilets during my breaks, praying that they wouldn't guess where I was. Teachers sometimes came to my rescue, but as soon as their backs were turned, the taunts started again. Miserably, I would wonder what it was about me that roused my classmates to dislike me so much.

Chapter Fifty-five

Maybe each believing that the other had informed me of some of the rudimentary facts of life, neither Sue nor my grandmother had told me about periods. I was eleven when searing stomach cramps woke me early one morning; doubled up with pain, I forced myself to get out of bed and go to the toilet. Blood flowed into the bowl and I screamed in fear.

It was Sue who heard me and, to be fair, she lost no time in rushing up the stairs. 'What's the matter now, Sally?' she asked, with a look of irritation on her face, which disappeared when she saw my white face.

I could still feel the blood trickling out into the wad of toilet paper I had stuffed into my pyjama bottoms. 'I'm bleeding. Down there,' I told her, indicating approximately whereabouts.

'Oh, for heaven's sake, has no one told you about periods?' she asked. Then, seeing my confusion, she realized they hadn't.

For once she showed me some kindness. She sat me down with a warm drink and two aspirins. She then explained that this was something that would happen to me each month. 'I suppose you'll have to take the morning off school. I've not got anything to give you,' she said, which I later learnt meant that she didn't have any sanitary towels, which she would have thought more suitable for a girl of eleven than the tampons she used. The annoyance returned to her voice when she said she would have to go to the chemist.

She phoned the headmaster, and I squirmed with embarrassment at the idea of him knowing. Then, again showing some sympathy, she gave me a hot-water bottle, told me to stay in bed until my cramps had subsided, and drove off to the chemist. On her return she showed me how to wear a sanitary belt and gave me a packet of mauve-paper-wrapped towels.

Although she had said I should go to school in the afternoon, she allowed me to stay at home for the rest of the day. The next morning when I went back to school I was terrified that somehow the children would be able to tell what had happened. My fears were realized when one curious child looked in my briefcase and saw two spare towels tucked behind my schoolbooks. If I had thought they'd mocked me before, it was nothing to what I had to put up with then. I became the butt of more jokes.

It took several more months before their teasing brought down the wrath of the headmaster – not on them but on me. The bell had rung for the end of the last lesson and, picking up my briefcase, I had walked through the school gates.

Outside, a group of my classmates were standing giggling and somehow I knew that it had something to do with me.

'Here, Sally, look at this,' said one, as I tried to scurry past.

'Leave me alone,' I cried when, not wanting me to escape, the same boy grabbed my arm.

'Don't be in such a hurry – you'll want to see this.' He pushed me forward until I was looking at the school wall.

I felt my face flush when I saw what they were all laughing at. In big red letters were written the words 'Jimmy loves Sally East' and underneath was a large red heart.

Whoops of laughter came out of every throat. I tore myself away from my persecutors and walked off as fast as I could.

The next morning I hoped against hope that the red letters would have disappeared overnight but they were still there when I arrived.

The headmaster waited until the middle of my first lesson to show his displeasure. He came into the classroom and instructed me to follow him outside. As I walked to the door I could hear the barely repressed sniggers coming from the rest of the class.

Without explaining what he wanted, he marched me across the playground and through the gates, then stood behind me as again I was forced to look at the offensive writing. 'What is the meaning of this, Sally? Explain yourself.'

'I don't know, sir,' I replied. 'I didn't write it.'

'So why is it there? What's the meaning of it?'

'I think it means the opposite,' I replied sadly.

But there was no sympathy in the headmaster's face. 'Well, whatever you say, it's probably something you've done that's caused it. You can wash it off in your lunch break.' Then he marched me back to the classroom.

As soon as I had eaten in the canteen, a prefect brought me a bucket, scrubbing brush and a bottle of chemical cleaner. 'The head says you know what to do with them, so get to it,' he said, with a knowing grin.

Humiliated, I crossed the playground hearing more catcalls.

'What's the matter, Sally? Don't you like your message?' they shouted, and burst into loud, ridiculing laughter. I squared my shoulders and ignored the taunts until I got outside.

It took me that entire break to wash the wall and I used up more than half of the cleaning fluid. When I had finished I took the empty bucket back to the headmaster's office. 'Well, see that nothing like that happens again. You can go back to your classroom now,' were the only words he spoke to me and, unhappily, I did.

It was one of the teachers who finally sat me down and gave me my first lesson on survival. 'Sally, I know you get bullied,' he told me, 'but only you can put an end to it.'

'How do I do that, sir?' I asked, not believing anything would save me from it.

'Turn round and tell them to shut up. Bullies are cowards. Show them you don't care.'

'But I do,' I wailed.

'And they know it, Sally,' he answered. 'Think of some retorts to put them in their place so they're the ones who look foolish, not you. Then give it to them and walk off with your head held high. If you play the victim they'll do it more. You'll see, when they realize they're having no effect on you, they'll stop. Will you try it?'

'Yes, sir,' I replied, although I had little confidence that it would work.

I thought about his words that night, then remembered how Sue managed my father when he had done something to annoy her. She ignored him.

'Spotty,' yelled a child, the next day.

'Oh, don't be so stupid,' I retorted, copying one of Sue's often used phrases.

'Don't be so pathetic – can't you find someone your own size to pick on?' That was a good one to use on someone fatter, older or bigger than me.

'Leave me alone. I'm too busy to listen to your nonsense,' was another that worked with my tormentors.

By the end of a week I found that the teacher was right. Faced with my seeming indifference and the snubs I'd stolen shamelessly from Sue's repertoire, the teasing eventually stopped.

As Sue had told me I would, I gradually grew into my uniform and, although my inability to participate in sports stopped me being popular, I was accepted.

I also tried to put my burgeoning self-confidence into practice at home. But I was no match for my father. The one thing I had learnt, though, was that victims were picked on and my pleas and cries excited him as much as the acts he made me take part in. I stopped the cringing and protesting. Instead I tried to show him the same weary contempt that had worked so well at school.

'What's the matter, Sally? Don't you love your daddy any more?' he would ask teasingly, when I looked coldly at him.

And, of course, even though I told myself I no longer did, I still wanted him to care for me.

'Good marks, Sally, well done,' he said, when my school reports arrived. And my cheeks would redden with pleasure. 'You're my special girl, aren't you, Sally?' he would still say on other occasions and, despite my intention to ignore him, I would find myself smiling back. 'Still a daddy's girl,' he would say when, after paying me a compliment, he saw pleasure reflected on my face. 'Got a kiss for your old man, have you? Or are you too old for that now?' Under the gaze of a resentful stepmother, my lips would dutifully pucker up and a daughterly kiss would be planted on his cheek.

'That's my girl,' he would say, and over those years when I crossed from child to teenager, I was.

Chapter Fifty-six

Talk of what I was going to do when I left school started as soon as I turned thirteen. Did I want to train as a secretary? To which I hurriedly answered, no. Hotel work, maybe? But that also held no interest for me. Neither did any of the other careers that Sue and my father proposed.

'A nurse,' I said finally, for that profession came with an escape route from Sue and my father. No one pointed out that living in a nurse's home would mean that Dolly could not go with me. Instead they greeted the idea with enthusiasm. 'Working on the children's wards or even with babies?' said a misty-eyed Sue, who still dreamt of a baby of her own.

To please her I said, 'Yes.' But it was not until I was fourteen that I decided what I really wanted to do when I left school.

I was eager for more pocket money so Sue and her father had persuaded me to work at the local old people's home. Because of my age I was only allowed to be a part-time helper, but the very low wages such a job paid still made me feel rich. Sue's father knew the matron and had recommended me to her. He was a self-made man, as he told me repeatedly, who had started work in the building industry when he was only a year older than I was then. He had never forgiven me for the lies I had told four years earlier, and advocated hard work and serving others as a way of redeeming my reputation and preparing for the future. 'Hard work never harmed anyone,' was his mantra, an ethos that did not seem to extend to his own daughter. 'It'll make you less introverted too, Sally,' he said. 'It'll get you to see how the real world works instead of daydreaming with your head stuck in some book.'

I felt like retorting that his daughter was the reason I spent so much time alone, and that it was Sue who had made me look different when I was sent to the new school. I wanted to scream out that it had taken nearly all of the four years I had been there to be grudgingly accepted. I could also have said that because I wanted to do well in my end-of-term exams, which would have pleased him, my studious behaviour had earned me the label 'swot' and 'teacher's pet' and that yet again I was subjected to teasing and ridicule. But I decided wisely that silence would benefit me more.

So, instead of voicing my thoughts, I smiled my thanks when he said he had arranged an interview for the following day.

The matron, a tall, rather thin woman with deep-set brown eyes and short dark hair shot with grey, seemed delighted that I was happy, during school holidays and at weekends, to work with the elderly. She asked me a few questions, such as what I wanted to do when I left school, which subjects interested me, and why I was interested in working there. A picture of my grandmother came into my head and I replied that I liked old people. Her rather stern demeanour changed as she smiled warmly at me. After explaining what my duties would be – helping with bedmaking, pushing round the trolley at mealtimes and anything else one of the permanent staff asked of me – she promptly arranged some shifts.

It was on a Saturday just a few weeks before Christmas that I started working there. Every house I passed already had its decorations up and some even had fairy-lights adorning the trees outside and hanging round their doors and windows.

The old people's home was in a rambling Victorian building that many years before, when large families had a bevy of servants, had been occupied by just one family. In the fifties it had been turned into a residential home for the elderly and now it also housed people who had become too feeble to care for themselves. It looked from the outside as though Christmas was passing it by. Unlike its neighbours there were no coloured lights woven in the trees; nor could I see any decorations through the windows. The large front garden, which in summer would be a blaze of colour when the flowers were in full bloom, now only contained drooping shrubs and empty beds. It looked brown and drab. There were sturdy wooden benches on the leaf-strewn grass and I imagined how it would look when the sun shone on the elderly people who would stroll out there to sit and watch the world go by. In the gloomy winter light the house had a shuttered appearance, as though the people who lived there had long ago ceased to love it.

I had been told to arrive mid-morning, just as 'elevenses' was being served.

'You can push the trolley and help serve tea. It's a good way to meet the residents,' I was told. As I wheeled it along the overheated corridors it was the smell that I first became aware of. Like other institutions and hospitals I had been in, there was the pervading one of disinfectant and overcooked cabbage but underneath it the acrid smell of urine and used bedpans.

'Let's get the worst over with first,' said the young carer, who had been charged with showing me round. I pushed the trolley into the frail care ward where the weakest of the residents were. Some lay against the pillows with their eyes closed and their mouths open, and it was only the sound of their breathing that told me they were still alive. They were passing their final days in a semi-conscious trance and I hoped that their dreams were of happy times. I watched nurses holding baby-style feeding cups to sunken toothless mouths. Cracked lips smacked, dribbles ran down chins and were wiped away. Occasionally a withered arm would stretch out and the bed's occupant would wave away the white-uniformed carer and insist they were strong enough to hold the cup for themselves.

My next stop was the lounge where the more mobile sat watching television. Strands of gold and green tinsel were strung around the room and in the corner stood a huge Christmas tree decorated with streamers, a few stars and a rather dilapidated angel that teetered on the top. Christmas cards from relatives and a few surviving friends hung on a string in front of the fireplace.

I was greeted with smiles and thanks as aged spotted hands brushed against mine when I passed cups of sweetened tea and the biscuits, which were immediately dunked in the cups. It was when I looked into the faded eyes shining out of the creased faces that I felt a special kind of warmth: they were so grateful to me for doing what I considered was so little.

So many inhabitants and so few visitors, I thought, over the days I worked there. I witnessed their delight when they received a Christmas card or a letter, and never heard a bitter word said about their absent offspring who seldom visited – even at special times of year. 'They're very busy' or 'They live so far away' were the excuses I heard time and time again.

As I got to know them, I grew fond of them, and much of my hard-earned cash went on buying small presents for everyone I knew was going to remain there for the festive season. Some of the more sprightly were going to their families for a few days. They had talked to me with excitement of seeing their children, grandchildren and even great-grandchildren. They repeated to themselves the exact time that they were being picked up, and recited greedily the details of what they would have to eat. Old eyes shone as if the telling reassured them that they were not forgotten.

They also told me stories of their distant families. Treasured photographs were held out in trembling fingers for me to admire. Excuses for their family's long absences were uttered in a vain hope that perhaps they, too, would believe them.

They tended to dwell far more in the past than the present. As I listened to them I tried to imagine the people they had once been, when their faces had been unlined, their hair thick and glossy and their limbs supple. Some recounted stories from their youth. They had lived in a time before the war, and they told how their lives had changed when the Prime Minister had grimly informed the nation that Britain was at war. Rheumy eyes dampened as, with faraway expressions, they talked of the young men who had left, never to return, and the camaraderie that the tragedy of war had brought.

'They were the best years of my life,' said one, and I wondered, as I saw other heads nod in agreement, how they could think that, given that bombs had flattened whole areas of the north, extinguishing many lives decades before their time. But it was the comradeship they had missed when it ended and the opportunities that those years had given them. For the war not only heralded the end of the class system, but the need for land and factory workers meant that women were no longer told that their place was in the home. It was during those years that women of all ages had tasted the sweetness of independence and a sense of self-worth.

I thought of Sue's father telling me I spent too much time with my head in my books. Here, I was listening to volumes of stories, told especially for me.

There were some, of course, who had turned into children trapped in an old person's body. I only hoped that if I lived to their age I would not be caught for ever in childhood memories. But at fourteen that seemed too far away to imagine.

I volunteered to work on Christmas Day. On Christmas Eve I tied up my tiny parcels with rolls of brightly coloured paper and gold string, then wrote the names on the cards. Edna, Violet, Edith, Ray and Joe, all names from a different era than my own. I was rewarded with smiles and delight as the paper was removed and, with the practice that years of frugality had engendered, carefully folded and put to one side to be reused on another occasion, should they live to see it. I felt my face stretch into a wide smile when I watched the reactions to my gifts. Delicately scented lavender soap was held up to the noses of frail old women, and fine cotton lawn handkerchiefs, which once their generation had treasured, were enthusiastically admired before being placed on their bedside tables with the card. Old men with badly fitting dentures, or none at all, sucked noisily on the boiled sweets I had parcelled up, and effusive thanks rang in my ears as I was told over and over that my gifts were exactly what they wanted.

I stayed on to help serve the Christmas lunch – thin slices of turkey, with thick gravy and mashed potatoes. Taking into consideration loose dentures and toothless gums, the vegetables were also mashed and easy to spoon in. I pulled crackers and placed paper hats on heads where the hair was so thin the scalp was visible and stayed until silence was called for and the radio turned up loud for us to listen to the Queen's speech.

It was that Christmas when I decided what I wanted to do. I wanted to train as a carer and spend my time with people who were reaching the end of life, not those who were just entering it.

I made one friend there who was not much older than I was and who, like me, had not been happy at home: her inability to pass exams had enraged her parents. She was a tall, gangling girl with red hair and freckles and her pale myopic eyes looked seriously at me from behind the thick lenses of her glasses.

It was she who introduced me to another world – the one of citizen's band radio. Like today's Internet chat rooms, the old-fashioned clumsy device, which we thought was so modern, could connect us to far-flung countries as well as neighbouring towns. It was our way of talking to strangers and reinventing ourselves as anyone we wanted to be. I saved up the money from my weekend work until I could purchase my own set. Hidden in my room, it came out in the evening as I talked to other isolated and lonely people, truck drivers and those in search of cheap dates.

It was then that I remembered my childhood daydreams of being popular, where friends hung on my every word, of standing on a stage listening to admiring applause, of being successful, of feeling important. All those fantasies could, for a short time, be brought alive when I talked on the radio into the night. In turn I was a secretary in a large company, a model who was tired of only being dated for her looks and occasionally, just occasionally, I was me, Sally.

They asked to meet me, those men I talked to late at night. I refused: I didn't want to spoil my imaginary adventures.

I left my father's house a few months after I had taken my GCE exams – not to work in the home where I had been for two years but at one in another town. I wanted to put distance between Sue, my father and myself. Surprisingly, when I told my father that I was leaving he made no protest.

'Well, you're a woman now,' he told me, with that lopsided smile of his. Then he added, 'I helped to make you one, didn't I, Sally?' He gave me some money and, just as when I was younger and he had cuddled me after doing terrible things to me, I felt the same conflicting emotions that being near to him always gave me. That yearning for the old father and the hatred for the cruel and abusive man I knew him to be.

I quickly found a bedsitter and permanent work, using the glowing reference that the matron had given me. For companionship I had my radio and, of course, faithful little Dolly who, at ten, adapted to her new quarters very quickly.

When I left home at nearly seventeen, I thought that at last I was free – free of my father, his threats and his control – but I wasn't. Just his 'daddy's voice' on the phone, when he played the role of the concerned father, was enough to transport me back to my childhood. No: freedom took another twenty years to arrive.

The CB radio was my salvation and my companion: on it I could talk to lonely strangers in the darkness of the night. Our anonymity gave us the confidence that life had failed to do, and we talked with the ease that so often strangers have with one another when they believe that they will never meet again. In our case we were even more protected for should we pass each other in the street, we would do so unknowingly.

Along the way loneliness made me break my rule twice when I arranged to meet those strangers. At seventeen I chose a brightly lit wine bar where the fluorescent lighting and the crowd of jostling people made me feel safe. At thirty it was the bar of a large hotel. Twice I heard the words 'You're special,' and the need to hear them more often was the reason I married, over a period of thirteen years, both of those men. My first husband was a sweet young man who said he adored me and gave me two children, before my inability to love him in return drove him away.

The second man was tall and blond, with a winning smile. He took in me and my two children, asked me to marry him and smiled with joy when I said yes. Watching me showering love on my small daughter and son, for their youth made them defenceless and thus incapable of hurting me, he pleaded with me to show that I also cared for him. I told him I did for I could only use words to show him my feelings. When frustration turned his pleas into shouts of rage I left him.

'Selfish,' both of my husbands said. 'Cold, unfeeling and ungrateful,' were the last accusing words they uttered before the front door shut and I was left standing in the quiet, a captive of my fears. Love, I had found, given to the undeserving, can turn into a weapon wielded by a monster.

It was when I finally received a phone call that I had not been expecting that the glimmer of freedom beckoned.

'Your father is dead,' said Sue.

'Our father is dead,' said Billy.

'I'm not coming to the funeral,' was my reply.

Instead on that day I sat alone in a bar and ordered a drink. As I thought of his body being lowered into the earth I tried to remember the man he had once been, the one I had loved.

But the other memories crowded in; the ones that I had for so many years pushed into the recesses of my mind. I heard his voice, saw his conspiratorial smile and remembered more than anything my fear. But still I whispered goodbye.

For a week I went to the same bar, took a book and tried to look nonchalant. I didn't want to talk to anyone but I needed to be around the warmth of strangers. The barmaid came to me on a night when pouring rain had kept her customers away.

'What's wrong, dear?' she asked me. 'I've seen you sitting here with your book, but the pages don't get turned, do they?'

'My father has just died. The funeral was only last week,' I told her.

'Are you sad because you miss him?' she enquired.

'No, because I don't.'

She said nothing to that, and only gave me a reflective look from blue eyes that had lost their customary sparkle. 'I see,' she said, and I wondered if she did.

After that I ordered another drink, then another – oh, not enough to be really drunk but just enough for euphoria to come. I got into my car and that's the last thing I remember of that night. The next day I woke up in hospital. I had laughed at the police, I was told, when they managed to stop my speeding car. Whatever they said I kept laughing and laughing, and I was still laughing when the medics arrived – I couldn't stop. They had contacted my husband, a nurse said.

'He's gone,' I replied, although I didn't really grasp her words. But the police had searched my bag for identification and found something with his address on it. He came to see me. He said he would come back; maybe treatment would help my coldness. I sent him away.

Once he had gone I cried. Then, as I had done the night before, I laughed. It mixed with my tears and I couldn't stop. Harsh and loud, it bounced off the walls until nurses came and I was given an injection.

The next day a doctor visited me. He sat by my bed and asked me questions. What had happened to me? Did I even remember being brought into the hospital? I turned away, my shoulders shaking with the sobs of the child I had once been.

I was transferred then. I needed a different sort of help, they said, as they took me to a ward with putty-coloured walls. There, blank-eyed people stared out of windows at sights only they could see.

'Breakdown' was the word I heard, when tablets were handed to me. Why now? I asked myself. Why now, when he's gone?

I had therapy and drugs, but I still couldn't tell them the reason I was there or describe the feeling of being cast adrift and explain my loneliness.

My children, now teenagers whose schooldays were behind them, came to visit, patted my hand and gave me flowers. They looked much as I must have done when I was a child visiting my mother in a similar room: uncomfortable.

I asked for cigarettes, and once all the visitors had left, the other patients and I went to the smoking lounge. We were as relieved to see them go as they were to leave. Conversation was spasmodic as, lost in our own thoughts or in some drug-induced calm, we sat with the wreaths of smoke swirling around our heads.

Gradually, as the days passed, as though they were

drawn by some inexplicable force, a small group gathered around me. There were hesitant smiles, desultory conversation started and, knowing there was a purpose to their closeness, I waited for one to tell me what it was.

The first to tell her story was Bridie, a young Irish girl who had fled her home just a few years prior to her admission to the hospital; a girl younger than most whose arms bore the scars of the self-harmer. She turned to me as she told it, and as I listened to her lilting accent, and prompted her with the odd question I was transported into her story.

Her tale took me to Ireland, and as I went with her to that mist-covered island, I saw it through her eyes, a cold place steeped in narrow-minded bigotry, and I seemed to hear an Evangelist minister as he preached of hellfire and damnation. Her hypnotic voice introduced me to her harsh stepfather, a man who had ruled his small household with a rod of iron, a man who believed that women were second-class citizens and that every child is born with sin. Finally she led me into the world that had become hers within weeks of her mother, a widow, marrying her second husband. It was a world I understood, the world of the abused child.

At night when the lights had been dimmed and I lay listening to the disturbed sounds of others' sleep, I reflected on Bridie's story. I asked myself why she had wanted to confide in me. Is there a secret badge we wear, a mark only visible to one who belongs to the same group? I learnt over the course of the next few weeks that often we did recognize ourselves in the faces of people we met. We know that they also are the ones: the ones whose families destroyed their childhood before casting them aside without direction.

It is on days when we are troubled that we become aware of our lack of roots. Those roots that keep others secured firmly to the ground are missing in us. We, who were never nurtured when young, drift aimlessly when faced with the storms of life. It is then that we find each other, sometimes fleetingly when help is needed; at others we can bond for ever.

Had Bridie seen past the woman of nearly forty I was to find the vulnerable child I had once been? I thought she had.

'It was my uncle,' said another woman, when our nightly ritual of lighting our cigarettes and savouring the first drag took place.

'It was my Scoutmaster,' said a man.

But I said nothing.

Neither did a pale-faced man: completely withdrawn, he sat with us each night but seldom spoke.

'He's on suicide watch,' I was told, when I asked why a nurse was seldom far from him. And I wondered what his story was. But deep down I already knew.

I listened to the stories of others but still I said nothing and neither did the man on suicide watch. But as the days slipped by I found my gaze settling on him more and more. What, I wondered, had driven him to such despair that he needed to be watched so closely?

It was several days after Bridie had told her story that, as though by some unspoken command, our fellow smokers rose and left us alone together. Then Jim, as I had learnt his name was, finally spoke. 'It was my father,' he said. And my hand stretched out and gently touched his.

He told me of beatings with steel-buckled belts and ham-sized fists, of broken bones and cracked ribs. How as he grew, so had his rage. But, too small to vent his anger on the six-foot drunk who had fathered him, he chose boys of his own age to fight. The school complained to the parents and the beatings increased. At sixteen he ran away, and at seventeen he did what so many troubled boys did: he enlisted in the army.

He was posted to Germany. His need to find love led him into a marriage with a woman who, having gained a rent-free home, rewarded him with first a daughter, then unfaithfulness. He stayed, for he loved his child, but when he was posted back to England, his wife refused to accompany him. He wrote begging her to follow him. His letters came back with 'not known at this address' stamped on them. It was then he knew he had lost his daughter.

He went to see his father and to confront the man who had destroyed his childhood. Instead of the six-foot brute he remembered, he found a gaunt old man with the yellow-tinged face and the deep cough of the terminally ill.

Three months later he paid for his father's funeral, then walked away from the woman who had watched her husband's brutality without protest. His father's death had not set him free either. He mourned his lost childhood and the daughter he would never see again. It was then that he had lost the will to live. 'And you?' he asked.

'My father too,' I answered, and for the first time I told my story. Not all of it then, but little bits at a time until finally he knew the whole.

It was in the telling that I gained my freedom from the past, and his listening that woke something in me and thawed my coldness. It was then that, instead of seeing merely a man, I saw a kindred spirit. We talked into that night and the nights that followed – and the nurses watched us.

Relationships between patients were not encouraged because they knew we were vulnerable. But from our vulnerability grew strength. I was there for six months and I was discharged first. Jim stayed a little longer. I visited him every day, and when he was discharged he came to me.

We had been together for three years, during which I learnt what love was and felt the joy of being able to return it, before I told him there was a place I needed to go back to.

Chapter Fifty-seven

It was a bright summer's day when I made my journey to the cemetery. My arms were full of gladioli, their bright petals resting against my jumper as I inhaled their light, peppery scent. The white flowers of the mountain ash mingled with the deep green of the yews growing in abundance around the edges of the graveyard. A light summer breeze rustled the leaves, making them cast dancing shadows over the pathways. I could hear Jim's footsteps as he kept pace with me. I had no need to hear him speak: his presence was enough. My feet took me past the ornate headstones where sightless statues kept watch over those who rested there. I paused at one, where a child's teddy bear, its colour faded by the elements, lay propped against a white headstone, and shivered at the thought of the unknown parent's grief.

Continuing around a bend I saw the pond where brown, green and white ducks, their young following, glided contentedly across its surface. Finally we came to the headstone I was looking for. On a nearby bench sat an old man. His lips moved as words unheard by humans left his mouth. His feet, clad in well-polished brown brogues, were set firmly on the ground and a walking-stick was held loosely in his age-spotted hands. The day was warm, and I noticed he was smartly dressed in grey flannel trousers, a navy blue wool jacket and a black tie knotted under his starched white collar. A crisp white handkerchief showed at the edge of his breast pocket and his sparse grey hair was combed neatly back from his face.

For a few seconds I thought he must be someone I knew and that the words I couldn't hear were directed at me. Then I realized that his eyes were fixed on a fresh grave; one where the headstone had not yet been erected. Without speaking I sat beside him.

He turned his face with its faded blue eyes under creased lids towards me. 'Just because we can't see someone it doesn't mean they're not here,' he said.

'No,' I replied, thinking of the many times I had believed that.

I felt the warmth of Jim's arm slide around my shoulders as I looked at that other grave, on which the writing on the headstone had only spread to two lines: 'Laura East, loving wife and mother', and the date she had died. A vase, from which the water had long since evaporated, stood in the centre. The brittle brown stalks of the spray of baby's breath and freesias, the last flowers I had placed there, seemed to reproach me for my long absence. I knelt beside it and stroked the cool purple-streaked stems of the gladioli before laying them on the grave. 'I searched for her for so long,' I said. 'Every day I would wait for her to come back but she never did. Sometimes I saw her in the street, just a glimpse of long fair hair, a curve of a cheek, or a brightly coloured skirt swirling in the breeze. But when I called her name the face turned to me was never hers.'

And again I felt the loneliness of abandonment I had known so very long ago.

I saw out of the corner of my eye the tears on the old man's face as he talked to his wife. Then a faint smile lifted the corners of his mouth – a memory of the good times had consoled him. As if he had sensed my thoughts, I heard Jim murmur in my ear, 'Sally, just keep remembering the good times,' and I smiled up at him with gratitude, for it was thanks to him that I was now able to.

That last time, four years earlier, when I had knelt silently by the grave, the ghost of my childhood had wrapped icy fingers around mine and led me back to a place I wanted to forget – a place where my mother ignored me for days at a time and I was Daddy's special little girl.

That day I had been unable to separate the good memories from the bad. However hard I tried to see a happy picture in my mind, it was obscured by a sad one. But over the days, weeks and months since then I had learnt how to put the good ones in front.

I sat beside the grave, told her silently that I still missed her, but unlike the old man, I knew she was really gone. The air chilled as the sun faded from the sky and Jim pulled me gently to my feet. 'Let's go home, Sally,' he said. Together we walked back past the pond where, with their heads tucked under their wings, the ducks had turned into floating silken cushions, along the moss-covered paths until we reached the iron gates of the entrance. Still with Jim's arm around my shoulders, we walked out through them into the noise of traffic.

read more

TONI MAGUIRE

CAN'T ANYONE HELP ME?

An inspirational true story of struggle and survival against all odds, co-written by the queen of misery memoirs, Toni Maguire.

Unwanted as a baby and abused by a paedophile ring from early childhood, Jane spent her youth trapped in a never-ending nightmare.

Under the watch of her uncle, she was habitually tied up and molested, beaten, burnt by cigarettes and urinated on. At twelve Jane escaped from reality by sniffing glue and after some years she graduated to heroin. Rejected by her mother, she was placed in a home for disturbed children and subsequent bad relationships resulted in the birth of two children.

She was thirty before she sought professional help and after weeks of agony in rehab, Jane succeeded in kicking her habit.

It was then that she turned her life around.

This book will be published in July 2011